The Art of Tile

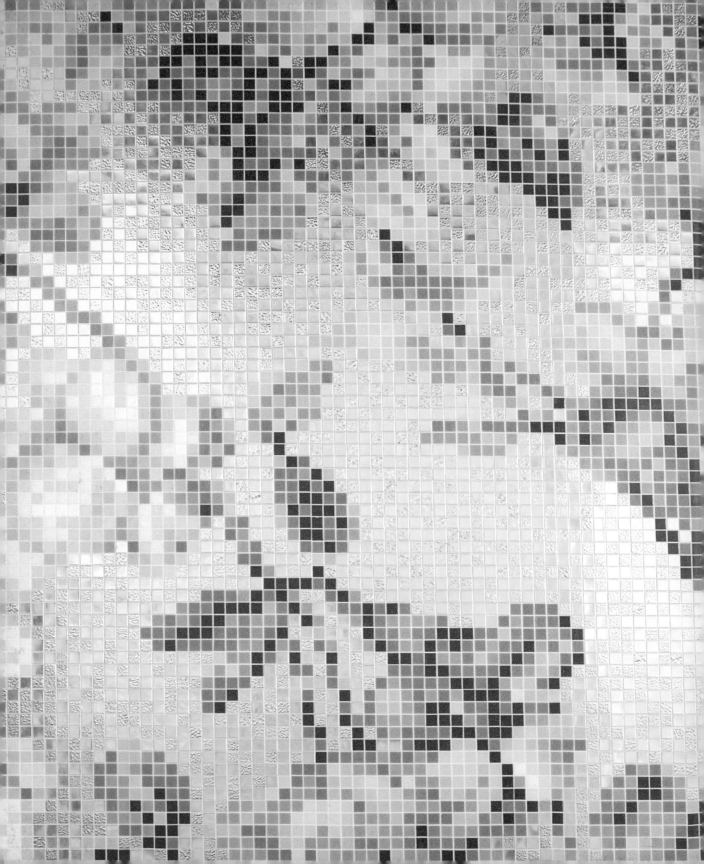

The Art of Tile

Designing with Time-Honored and New Tiles

Jen Renzi

Photographs by Ben Ritter

Clarkson Potter/Publishers
New York

Published in the United States by Clarkson Potter/Publishers, an imprint of the Crown
Publishing Group, a division of Random House, Inc., New York.
www.crownpublishing.com
www.clarksonpotter.com

Clarkson Potter is a trademark and Potter with colophon is a registered
trademark of Random House, Inc.

Library of Congress Cataloging-in-Publication Data
Renzi, Jen.
The art of tile: designing with time-honored and new tiles / Jen Renzi ;
photography by Ben Ritter.—1st ed.
Includes index.
1. Tiles in interior decoration. I. Ritter, Ben. II. Title.
NK2115.5.T54R46 2009
747'.9—dc22   200801753

ISBN 978-0-307-40691-0

Printed in China

Design by Wayne Wolf/Blue Cup Creative
Photographs by Ben Ritter

10 9 8 7 6 5 4 3 2 1

First Edition

For Ginger and Bobby

Contents

the options

Introduction

Whether you're new to tile or have long been seduced by its charms, now is the perfect time to bring it home with you. Famously low maintenance, durable, and easy to clean, tile is an enduringly popular choice—think of chic slate squares gracing an entrance hall, or a frieze of sprightly Mexican ceramics brightening a fireplace. But lately, tile has shed its reputation as just a sturdy and practical design solution. A tiled surface can be a piece of artistry, too—as can individual tiles themselves. In the last few years we have witnessed a watershed in tile's decorative use in spaces ranging from traditional Shingle-style cottages to avant-garde lofts. As the vogue for open-space living has dissolved walls between kitchen and living area and between bedroom and bath, tiles are moving from the back of the house to center stage; they are perfectly suited to stitching spaces together both functionally and aesthetically. Home owners have been emboldened to use flower-print mosaic accent walls in dens, Pop Art–patterned floors in entrance halls, and even stone-tiled headboards. Tile's expressive potential has been unleashed.

Coinciding with—or perhaps the spark behind—such design innovation, the world of tile has exploded. An abundance of stunning options in a wide array of finishes, shapes, textures, sizes, and materials, from circular stainless-steel penny tile to tinted-cement hexagons, allows designers and home owners unlimited creative freedom. Top manufacturers like Ann Sacks, Bisazza, Artistic Tile, and Walker Zanger continually push the envelope with their offerings, developing tiles that rival wallpaper in their juicy patterning, with bright colors and bold oversized motifs like toiles and damasks. They're also expanding availability and variety in formerly specialized materials—like quartz agglomerates and sustainable coconut—and textures, offering tiles with groovy ripples and ridges.

Opposite: **Striking a restful note, the soothing coloration of French limestone pavers reflects daylight filtering into a sunny courtyard. A circular swath of small tiles set into the larger square stones creates the effect of an area rug.**

9

Technological advancements in tile production have increased the places where and ways in which tile can be used while enhancing its aesthetics. Leathers now come with eco-friendly, stain-resistant coatings and with magnetized backing systems for ease of replacement. Metal, often favored for decorative inserts within a field of stone or ceramic, is coming into its own as an all-over surfacing material offered in sizes from bronze mosaics to large-format aluminum squares. Sophisticated digital printing produces tough-as-nails porcelains that look exactly like sheets of beautifully patinated Cor-Ten steel, woven sisals, or button-tufted upholstered walls. Improvements in mold-making have aided the creation of oversize tiles that are lighter and thinner than their predecessors, and thus suitable for walls and ceilings. Stain-resistant grouts come in every color of the rainbow. And river rocks and mosaic, which once required painstaking hand placement, are available as modular mesh-backed squares for easier, less expensive installation. Porcelain tiles impregnated with chemical enhancers clean impurities from the air, while acrylic tiles embedded with fiber-optic lights bring a bit of sparkle to the backsplash. Even age-old traditions like handcrafted cement are flourishing courtesy of a yen for products made using sustainable methods and bearing the personal imprint of their maker.

But the exciting expansion of the tile market makes it that much harder to navigate. Most people don't know where to start with tile and don't know how to design with it once they've narrowed their selection. Plus, the stakes seem so high. Tile's permanence—one of its coveted attributes—also makes it difficult to switch out every few years, unlike fabrics or wallpaper. Thus, too many home owners avoid designs with a powerful impact in favor of playing it safe with subdued colors and materials.

That's where this book comes in. While offering a comprehensive survey of today's hottest, chicest, and most time-honored tiles, this all-in-one guide prepares you for immersion in this vast material landscape and gives you the tools to dive deeper on your own. It offers insight from those who've installed (and lived with) tile in their own homes as well as the advice of professionals who make, sell, or design with it. Fear or ignorance is no longer an excuse to default to white subway tile!

Guiding you through the entire process, from selection to maintenance, this sourcebook explains how to think about tile, arming you with vital information needed to make an informed choice and showing you the steps for moving forward once you've fallen for a particular option. We start big—with whole houses and innovative rooms—and then tighten the focus on details like corners and trims that help you achieve a finished, sophisticated look. Page after page of individual tiles will help you determine the sort of visual impact you hope to make and then lead you down the right path so you can rule out certain options and gravitate toward others.

"Designing with Tile" addresses context, explaining the fundamental principles of color, pattern, and texture and their impact on your search. For inspiration, we access the inner sanctums of myriad design mavens across the globe, from Marrakech to Miami, who have built their homes and lives around tile.

Tiles can bring color, pattern, and texture to a room where it is lacking, or they can enhance attributes that already exist. Thanks to their versatility, you need not limit yourself when choosing where to install them. Wet space, dry space, heavily trafficked room, countertop, fireplace, tucked-away corner—a tile exists that's appropriate and appealing for all such environments. "A Performance Primer" outlines more practical matters, from the benefits and drawbacks of "living" materials like stone that patinate over time to how glazing affects structural integrity. Because tile's sturdiness and practicality are of no small importance to those seeking easier, lower-maintenance living, we offer a primer on materials so you understand which tiles can be used where and under what conditions.

"The Little Details" demonstrates how to compose a tiled surface and demystifies the varieties of trim pieces and borders. Learn how to treat corners and edges so your installation looks finished and showcases your chosen material to greatest effect. Determine ways in which grout can accentuate a tiled surface's graphic quality or let the material itself read as a continuous, unified swath. With so many grout colors on the market—even acid green, pale pink, and deep russet—grout has become a much more thrilling medium in its own right.

Of course, you'll want to know where and how to buy tile—and when this task is best placed in the hands of your decorator, builder, or contractor. This book presumes—and recommends—that you work with professionals rather than tackle tiling as a do-it-yourself project. Nonetheless, in "How It All Comes Together" we offer some insight into the installation process so you can understand how it will affect your selection.

The second part of the book consists of a catalog raisonné of more than a thousand tiles, grouped by material, genre, and design principles. Compare an embossed leather tile to one with a smoother surface. Get enthusiastic about the many ornamental eco-options at your disposal. Become awed by the breadth of stone. Marvel at the bounty of textured relief tiles. Be enticed by the splendid array of mosaics and murals.

The book concludes with lists of myriad resources, from large international showrooms to specialty makers, to jump-start your search. You'll find installers, trade associations, and other services to educate you further about this bountiful and exciting genre.

Opposite: **Dressing up the walls of a bathroom, glamorous large-scale porcelain tiles glazed with a painterly tone-on-tone damask pattern mimic the look of wallpaper or an exquisite silk fabric.**

This book encourages you to define and refine your own needs and aesthetic. Experiment, unleash your creativity, and open your eyes to the expressive potential of tile. And as long as you address the practicalities of installation, do your research, and collaborate closely with your installer, you should feel liberated to follow your own tune. Play with the options and celebrate the joy of putting your personal imprint on your home.

DEFINING TILE

A quick note before we get started: What, exactly, is tile?

Tile is as much a method as a material. Some think of tile as only ceramics. Indeed, when I was researching this book, people would often ask me whether I planned to include natural stone or whether I was extending the scope beyond stones and ceramic. My answers are yes and yes. First, tile is not limited to any specific material. These days we see cork tiles and cement ones, glass agglomerates and stone pavers, mosaics made of wood and stainless steel. There are leather tiles and rubber tiles. In this book, I have even included resin-based tiles that stick to the wall with Velcro (above).

Tile can be described as any material that is installed in a modular format and adhered to, rather than just laid upon, a substrate. Within this definition, tiles can come in all shapes and sizes, from ¼-inch mosaics to 24 by 36-foot large-format porcelains. Additionally, tile serves both a functional purpose and an aesthetic one—features that, in this case, go hand in hand.

Walls mosaiced in a pattern of subtle tonal checks in quiet shades of gray bring sophistication—and a dose of the unexpected—to a media room.

the big picture

With so many delectable materials, patterns, and motifs to choose from and such a rich history of cultural traditions to inspire you, the wide world of tile seduces and intrigues. But moving beyond just loving tile to really using it in your own home requires a crash course in the design basics, from hiring an installer to selecting the right color and pattern to achieve your desired look. Learn how to use tile as a building block of your décor, your aesthetic—and your life.

Designing with Tile

Perhaps you became intoxicated with the deep, water-color hues of a blue glass mosaic wall at a tile showroom, or the rough-hewn striations of tumbled limestone tiles caught your eye. The vibrancy of Spanish polychrome might have left an impression during a trip to Barcelona, or you've recently marveled at the intricate patterning of Middle Eastern tile work. Maybe you visited the home of a friend who'd clad a fireplace in Arts and Crafts–inspired ceramics drenched in mesmerizing glazes. Or perhaps your impending dining room renovation has sparked your curiosity about whether a boldly tiled floor or a single dramatic accent wall would be the better choice—and how it might look.

Somewhere along the way, you fell in love with tile and yearned to use it at home. But you're not quite sure *how*. The bounty of options at your disposal—from candy-colored terrazzos to richly enameled lavastone—may breed confusion about which ones to choose and how to design with them. Does natural stone have any drawbacks? Can glass be used as flooring? Don't be discouraged. Even architects and designers often admit to lacking schooling in the subject and confess that they were forced to learn on their own about the subtleties of tile, mostly by scrutinizing vignettes in tile showrooms. (The good news, of course, is that you can do that, too.)

A perfect tile exists for every nook and cranny of your house and for any look you can envision. Finding the right kind is not the easiest task, but once you are primed with solid guidance, you can enjoy the process as a delightfully fun treasure hunt.

Opposite: Gail Shields-Miller used lush Spanish limestone throughout her New York beach home—from the kitchen to the living area. Accented by a stripe of limestone stick mosaic, the elongated 24 by 4-inch tiles are reminiscent of wood planks. "Unusually sized materials have a tremendous design impact, making a simple floor plan look more dynamic and textured," the designer explains.

Just perusing the bevy of available tiles is a crash course in finishes, motifs, and artisanal techniques, from hand-applying polychromes to tooling leather. You'll learn a lot about tiles and as much about material culture.

When you are searching for ideas and inspiration, understanding a few basic concepts and philosophies about tile will help decode this incredibly vast material category. First, consider tile in four dimensions. A single tile is an individual artwork

exhibiting unique physical qualities and character. A blue-and-white Delftware ceramic tile hand-painted with a sailboat recalls sixteenth-century Dutch living, for instance, while an etched-travertine border imparts a soulful Old-World presence. Second, tiles are modules, meant to be installed in a series. This feature invites you to indulge in pattern play and juxtaposition. Install hexagonal terra-cotta pavers for a rustic country French look, or alternate two contrasting colors of ceramic to suggest a sprightly checkerboard. Third, whether you are extending a swath of tile from the walls to the ceiling or insetting a grid of tile within a concrete floor, you can use tile to define spatial boundaries. Last, tile's durability ensures that it holds up well over time. Thus you must not only pick the right tile for the right application but also choose a color, finish, or glaze that inspires your unflagging adoration.

Above: **A practical alternative to wallpaper, compositional tiles feature a pattern that continues across a series of adjacent tiles—like these bold blooms on black porcelain.** *Opposite:* **A red-and-white mosaic in an abstract flower motif immerses an eating area in ornamentation. It covers three walls to intimately embrace diners, making the room feel like a world unto itself.**

You can start the design process by selecting a particular tile and building a space around it. Sometimes, after all, you cannot help but flip for a certain glazed terra-cotta or striated marble. But, more likely, you'll work from the opposite direction. You'll have in mind a certain location or aesthetic goal and then look for a tile to fulfill it. Thus the third dimension—how tile can create a sense of space—is a good place to begin.

Decoratively and spatially, think about tile in one of three ways. Tiles can create visual flow and unity from one room to another—or within four walls. Tiles can be used as a chic accent, playing off the surrounding décor or subtly emphasizing it in some way. Highlight an architectural feature—a stairwell, say, or a structural column. Or let tile perform as the main feature to design an entire room—or home!—around.

Continuity

Opposite: **French limestone pavers in the living area of a Coconut Grove home by Juan Carlos Arcila-Duque play off keystone wainscoting original to the 1920s house. The stones' even coloration provides a quiet backdrop for the owners' collection of fine art.**

Tile's unrivaled aesthetic and functional versatility makes it suitable for almost any living condition. Indeed, certain varieties are equally at home on walls and floors, indoors and out, in wet spaces and dry, in farmhouses and châteaux. Thus it's a natural fit for wherever you desire spatial unity or a pleasing visual flow between rooms. Make a bedroom and bath feel like an interconnected suite, or unify a kitchen and adjacent dining area. Similar tile can form an artful connective tissue between two zones.

Tile is especially ideal for open-plan spaces where sight lines extend from one corner of the house to another. When the palette or finishes change too drastically from room to room, those spaces can appear chopped up. Instead, choose the same or similar materials for walls or floors to create cohesion between adjacent spaces. Running limestone pavers or terra-cotta bricks in both, for instance, will stitch them together. It's the architectural equivalent of wearing the same color shirt and skirt—a continuous run of tile forms an unbroken line that also looks more tailored.

To create a fluid connection between the living spaces of a Coconut Grove home, for instance, designer Juan Carlos Arcila-Duque ran floor tiles of creamy French limestone throughout the lower level. The mellow coloration and tone nicely complement the existing wainscoting of heavily textured keystone walls, making the new floor seem integral to the house. Arcila-Duque used four different sizes of tile, from 6-inch squares to 12 by 24-inch rectangles, installed in a random pattern. The meandering geometry instills a casual vibe while breaking up the vast runs of the same material.

Throwing a curve into the otherwise clean-lined pattern of squares and rectangles, the house's courtyard centers on a large circular medallion—like a throw rug—that mixes smaller squares of limestone in two shades. The buttery material continues to the main living area, thus uniting them. "In the living room, I switched the limestone to twenty-four-inch squares, set in a grid so it's more formal and refined," the designer explains. The two zones are demarcated by insets of walnut planks, lending scale and variety to the room.

When uniting indoor and outdoor environments, your options are more limited. You'll need to choose a material that works well in both wet and dry, cold and hot conditions and, depending on the climate, one that's unaffected by frost. Stick with something sturdy like ceramic. For a more lived-in look, go for cement or certain

Juan Carlos Arcila-Duque mixed the tile size and pattern throughout this home, switching from a looser, irregular installation to a stricter grid in the open-plan living area. The 24-inch squares are inset with a band of walnut planks, like a carpet, to draw visual boundaries between the eating area and the adjacent sitting room.

Above: **To make a small Manhattan bathroom appear bigger, Peter Balsam limited himself to one material—transparent glass—for walls, floor, and shower, alternating the size and shape for variety.** *Opposite:* **Gail Shields-Miller continued the same Spanish limestone tiles used in her living room (page 18) into her dining area to unify the two spaces.**

natural stones, which weather beautifully over time. Slate or porcelain—more impervious to the elements while still offering plenty of visual variety—will work nicely, too.

You can also match tile to another material in adjacent spaces. If you can't bear continuing your dark-stained oak floorboards into your high-traffic kitchen, peruse the many options of woodlike porcelains instead; you can sometimes even match the tile size to the width of the wood planks. Because they are cut from such sturdy cloth, porcelains also pair well with natural stone or even leather in an adjacent room. So if you've splashed out on a luxurious leather-floored master bedroom and want to unify the space with your bath—where the material would be verboten—pick porcelain. Just stick with a similar color and finish.

Because your eye is drawn to them, floors offer the easiest route to a holistic décor. But don't forget the walls. A tile wainscot, chair rail, or baseboard repeated from room to room makes them feel continuous. You can even use the same tile to clad your backsplash and a nearby hearth so the two elements relate.

Tile contributes to creating continuity not just from one space to the next but *within* a space as well, a particularly effective trick to visually expand the proportions of smaller quarters. While surfacing walls and floor in different materials can give your eye something to move around, seemingly enlarging the dimensions, in most cases more unified surfaces offer the better route. Limit yourself to just one tile and play instead with pattern and texture.

Accent

Tile is a fabulous conduit for streamlining space and weaving together adjacent rooms. But because it comes in so many sparkling colors, fun motifs, and intriguing textures, you'll want to exploit its ability to instill liveliness and pep. Line a shelf in translucent glass, smooth over a windowsill in terra-cotta, encircle a doorway or a mirror in river-rock mosaic, install a continuous ceramic chair rail, or skim the inside of an archway between two rooms in azure Delftware. Clad the risers of a staircase to accentuate its zigzag lines, or frame the edge of a tub surround to bring a shot of color where paint wouldn't be wise. You can make a big statement with even a small swath of tile, as long as it's intelligently placed.

When creating an accent, you can use just one variety of tile, a complementary selection from the same collection or manufacturer, or a few styles mixed and matched. Many talented artisans craft murals—inventive pictorial compositions with patterning that extends across a number of tiles installed adjacent to one another. Some murals comprise just 3 or 4 tiles, others as many as 120—or more! While often inset into a field of a more subdued tile, usually in a color to match the background, a mural can also be positioned on its own as a self-contained decoration. Frame a mural within a recessed niche, or position one just above a mantel. Or liberate a mural from the constraints of an architectural feature and give it pride of place in the center of the wall, like an artwork.

In addition to highlighting an existing element like a fireplace or fountain, you can also create a feature out of tile itself. A swath of tile inset into the floor, like an area rug, carves out a little zone within a larger space, a sort of room within a room. An accent wall—a surface covered in top-to-bottom tile—offers another creative option. Pick the grandest wall in the room, such as the one backing your couch, or select a slim expanse between two doorways. An accent wall is particularly effective and enjoyable in spaces where the eye is less distracted by other activities and stimulation. Consider the plane behind the soaking tub or vanity of your master bath, a room encouraging leisure and contemplation. You can also convert the wall behind your bed into a feature wall, or tile just the lower half to create the illusion of a headboard.

Because walls are subject to fewer stresses like wear and scratching, almost any type of tile can be employed there. Choose ceramics, glass, or metal, or indulge in a decadent treatment like stained coconut, embossed leather, or mother-of-pearl. A limited canvas is a great excuse to showcase a pricey material that would be prohibitively expensive in a more expansive installation.

Opposite: **The empty wall behind a sink—whether in a small powder room or a grand master bath— provides the perfect excuse for an accent wall. Here, water-resistant porcelain tiles from Hastings in fun interlocking ovals lend spark to a simple white sink.**

Working at home is a joy when you have a vibrant mosaic wall of oversized flowers to keep you company. This Bisazza pattern, rendered in colorful glass, repeats over 51 inches. *Opposite:* Use tile to draw attention to an architectural element. A recessed niche becomes a major feature when dressed in translucent earth-toned glass mosaics that highlight the adjacent slate tiles and set off the objects on display.

Count mosaics among the most popular choices for accent walls, as the small size of the individual tiles, called *tesserae,* makes them easy to arrange into painterly lines and detailed imagery. Commissioning an artisan to tailor a unique installation to your exact specifications is a special gift to yourself and your home. Quite costly at times, yes, but worth it to live with an artist's touch and spirit.

Luckily, innovative manufacturers have made it even easier to bring home the custom look and the adventurous graphics of mosaics. Many now make high-impact patterns that come arrayed on modular sheets for easy installation, obviating the need for laborious (and costly) hand-placement of individual tiles on site. Choose between florals and geometrics, herringbones and stripes, modern styles and historic motifs evocative of the art form's Roman roots. You can even get winkingly clever designs that mimic the look of button-tufted fabric. Some companies also allow you to customize your own mosaic pattern; submit a photograph, and they will re-create the image in glass or ceramic to match your space constraints.

Consider going bold on a backsplash. Its typically narrow dimensions render it an ideal place to push design further than in other areas of the home. Although many confine a tiled backsplash to the sliver of space between the countertop and the upper cabinets, imagine extending it all the way to the ceiling, above the upper cabinet as well. Or run the pattern below the countertop and down to the floor below. The below-countertop area is often neglected, but when visible from surrounding rooms a tiled surface offers a nice, attentive touch.

A more traditional route is just as effective. Within a broader field, inset a medallion or a mural of a contrasting pattern for a little spunk. Choose from the many whimsical tiles printed with quirky food motifs, or create a more abstract play of color and shape.

The point of any accent—whether a shallow ledge or a full floor—is to make a statement. Don't be a wallflower; this is not the place for a restrained choice. But bold doesn't have to mean strong, assertive color. An intriguing material like shell, an unusual texture like leather, or a subtle finish that draws you in close can be just as effective.

1. Interior designer Nicole Sassaman surfaced a pair of wall niches flanking the entrance to her Malibu home with Jerusalem limestone mosaics. While the stone's coloration is quite subtle, the tiled surface has an inviting, rough-hewn texture that nicely complements the surrounding walnut woodwork. **2.** Tempering the harsh Florida sunlight, 4 by 16-inch blocks of gray-brown limestone from Trend form a headboard in a Miami Beach apartment. **3.** A bathroom is the perfect place to indulge your desire for a tiled jewel box. A walk-in shower striped in vibrant yellows, blues, and greens offers a perky morning pick-me-up.

1.

2.

3.

ACCENT WALLS

Above: To create a dramatic open kitchen for a Beverly Hills home, Jeff Andrews designed a back-splash of custom striped mosaic tiles, which come in 12-inch-square sheets backed by mesh. *Opposite:* The delicate bands of gold-leaf tile were inset by hand.

To revamp a cramped 1940s Beverly Hills bungalow, designer Jeff Andrews tore down as many walls as he could, refocusing the layout on an open kitchen. "Since it's in the center of the space, visible from all the living areas, I didn't want it to *look* like a kitchen," Andrews explains. "On the other hand, it still needed to *function* as a kitchen—while bringing cohesion to the décor."

So he decided to play with a wall of tile. A chic glass-mosaic backsplash extends from countertop to ceiling—

uninterrupted by upper cabinets—and doubles as a feature wall. The patterning is both lively and timeless. Tailored stripes, in an array of dark neutrals, are inset with slim hand-laid bands of gold-leaf tiles. The custom color combination meshes with the granite countertops, walnut floors, and white-lacquered cabinetry; stripes alternate between shades of copper, brown, ocher, black, and beige, offset with gray grout.

The glistening swath extends upward in an oh-so-subtle curve. "The ceilings are not super high, and there were no crown moldings to soften the transition between materials," Andrews explains. "The cove also gives the backsplash a less linear effect." Indeed, stripes aside, there's nothing straight-edged about the strong result—a functional backsplash that's also a work of art.

The Main Event

While tile can stylishly complement other furnishings or features in the home, it can also perform a starring role as the defining element of the décor. If you delight in playing with color, pattern, and atmosphere, then look to tile as the building block for an entire room or suite of spaces. Convert a master bath into a mosaic-clad fantasia, design a sunporch to double as a garden of hand-painted tile, or work from the ground up and let a floor paved in colorful geometric ceramics spark the interior of your entire living room.

An intense jewel box with every surface bedecked in tile offers a delightfully decadent interior. For historical precedents, look no further than Turkish hammams kitted out in head-to-toe tilework or the gilded mosaics of Roman churches. This level of intensity suits a small space like a stairwell or a dressing room with which you engage over shorter periods than you do the main living areas. Tiling every single surface—walls, floor, ceiling—makes sense in bathing areas, as the material is so suited to wet environments, especially in snug quarters where ventilation is an issue or in a walk-in shower that doubles as a steam room.

Less visually intense ways to make tile a decorative centerpiece include wainscoting walls and covering more than one surface with them. Take an accent wall a step further, wrapping it around to an adjacent wall for just a slightly more enveloping touch. Smooth over your entire floor in a spunky patterning, like a bold area rug; such a feature steals the show and begs to be the centerpiece of a room.

When making tile the main focus, let its color, glaze, or presence inform the surrounding elements. Choose fabrics, paints, and furnishings that complement rather than compete with it. Reiterate the pattern but in a slight variation—choose plaids to play off a checkerboard floor, for instance. Or riff off the character your tiles introduce—run with the French cottage theme suggested by rough-hewn terra-cotta pavers or imagine an Eastern-inflected Spanish confection for polychrome Malibu tiles.

At a Montauk home, for instance, architect James Biber envisioned a master suite floored entirely in 1960s op-art ceramic tiles. Enlivened by interlocking patterns of circles and diamonds, the tiles are perfect in a beachfront house that embraces sea and sky. The master suite was conceived to showcase the 20-centimeter-square tiles to greatest effect. An egg-shaped bathroom without doors divides the loftlike space, separating it into sitting and sleeping areas. Using partitions in place of walls and keeping the décor tailored puts the emphasis entirely on the slightly dizzying motif underfoot.

Opposite: **For a Montauk couple, architect James Biber designed a loftlike open-plan master suite divvied by an egg-shaped bathroom pod with no doors. He ran the tiles throughout the entire suite, creating an exuberant pattern underfoot. By using partitions in place of walls, he placed the focus entirely on the floor.**

Overlooking the ocean, a glass-walled crow's nest one flight above the sleeping area embraces the sea and sky. The geometric cerulean tile pattern was designed in the 1960s by Italian architect Gio Ponti; Biber had custom reproductions made to match vintage tiles in the clients' collection.

DESIGNING AN ENTIRE HOME AROUND TILE

Above: An 18th-century Marrakech *riad* unfurls around an open-air central courtyard. Samuel and Caitlin Dowe-Sands repaved the space in cement tiles of their own design, a zigzag motif arrayed in diagonal lines around the edge of the room and in a square format toward the center. (Be cautious when using the material out of doors, because it can be affected by frost and stained by water.)

A few years ago, Caitlin and Samuel Dowe-Sands left Los Angeles for Marrakech in search of adventure. They found it in the form of a crumbling *riad*—one of the centuries-old residences in the city's maze of twisting streets and narrow alleyways. The couple hadn't planned to set down roots, but rehabbing an old house in a foreign country seemed like a brilliant way to immerse themselves in its culture and local craft traditions.

The *riad*'s central courtyard—and the Marrakech climate—set the tone for the subsequent renovation. "The idea was to open things up—removing doors, adding windows, creating new doorways," Caitlin says. Spatial openness, however, equaled year-round exposure to the elements. So they decided to run sturdy floors of the same pressed cement tiles throughout the rest of the house, too.

Perusing the mom-and-pop tile makers in the neighborhood, they found the designs a bit historic for their taste. "One of the enchanting things about Morocco is the access to amazing artisans," says Caitlin. "You can design things to your own specifications and ignore all the rules." They started experimenting with looser graphics like loop-de-loops that took advantage of the soft, hand-drawn quality that distinguishes cement tiles. "We looked at the boldness of wallpapers and thought, Why not have a little fun with the floor?"

From any spot in the house you can see through the courtyard and into other rooms. To ensure that the design flowed harmoniously throughout, they used the same size and shape field tile—20-centimeter squares—and the same chalk-on-a-chalkboard palette as in the courtyard. "The rooms are quite small, so limiting the palette made them feel a little bigger," says Caitlin. Within those parameters, they played. Ribbons now loop through the living room. The breakfast nook is livened up by a more traditional grid with diamond-shaped insets. Abstracted floral medallions embellish the bathroom. A guest bedroom is clad in a pale coral print, forming a patterned headboard above the bed. The result is a house that feels unified but with plenty of variety and expansiveness.

1. With no doors to separate indoors and out, every room in the house has a view into the courtyard. To create continuity, Caitlin and Samuel used the same color tiles—graphite and white—switching the pattern from room to room.
2. A downstairs bathroom is outfitted in an abstract floral motif, reiterating the home's black-and-white theme to visually expand and unify the décor.

3. A pattern of graceful ribbons loops through the living room. The couple was so inspired by the process of customizing tiles for their home that they launched a company, Popham Design, to sell their creations.
4. A guest bedroom wall clad in coral-print cement tiles doubles as a headboard. This is the one room that departs from the black-and-white scheme, the pale gray palette softening the more intimate confines.

In the couple's eating nook, just off the kitchen, tiles take a backseat to bold red-painted walls. The pattern segues to a quiet grid of inky black squares, accented with chalky white insets. *Opposite:* In the living room, cool cement offers a surprisingly cozy touch. "The material wears beautifully," says Caitlin. "It keeps looking better as it gets walked on and scuffed." The couple experimented with various waxes and finishes like linseed oil, testing out the luster and feel underfoot. They settled on wax, applied with a cloth and then buffed.

Color

Tiles come in every color of the rainbow, from the sultriest violets to the most subdued blush, from opaque hues to translucent washes. With some materials—like many glass tiles, for instance—the color comes from the body of the tile and thus extends all the way through from top to bottom. In other cases, as with glazed ceramics or polychromed stone, the color comes from a surface treatment, like icing on a cake. Both the composition of the body and the character of the glaze affect the intensity of the hue.

When choosing color, you'll want to follow one of two avenues. Either the tile you pick will inspire the palette of its surroundings—in which case you're liberated to select whatever hue you flip for—or you will pick a tile color to play off a room's existing features. For example, replacing a backsplash or retiling a floor requires considering other aspects of the décor and selecting colors that complement them. When working around an existing scheme, you may want to bring swatches of fabrics and paint chips to the tile showroom to help guide your selection. And, because a color can change depending on its context—for example, a brightly illuminated showroom versus your more moodily lit living room—you should always check the color of your chosen samples in your home before committing.

When using tile as your starting point, narrow your options by thinking carefully about your overall design preferences. Do you desire a scheme that's bold or quiet? Do you prefer to use just a single color or to mix a few? Does a contrast of two hues sound like a good idea, or can you handle an even more active composition? Showroom salespeople and designers can provide invaluable assistance in zeroing in on a choice: Color is more an art than a science, with rules that are meant to be broken and blanket guidelines that don't always make sense for your particular situation.

In general, though, dark colors make a space seem smaller, while lighter colors open them up by pulling in light. Blues and greens are calming, and red and yellow offer an invigorating jolt. Whites and creams and earth tones are mellow neutrals that play well with others. Contrasting hues create an active composition, while complementary shades offer a more relaxed vibe. Mix many colors together and form groovy patterns, or balance just a touch of contrasting color within a field of another hue to lend scale to a broader swath.

Opposite: Dan Bleier brightened his New York apartment with a wall of colorful striped resin tiles of varying widths. To make the pattern less insistent, he confined it to a small side wall and slipped neutral cream stripes between the brighter hues.

Those yearning for powerful color may want to avoid stones—which have a beautiful coloration in their own right but tend to come in earthier hues—and steer toward glazed ceramics, cement, or glass. Or opt for a composite like terrazzo embedded with colorful chips of broken glass set against either a neutral background or an equally bold one.

Color doesn't have to mean bright. Dark brown and black may sound extreme, but both can be mysterious, moody, or quite classical depending on how they are used. A matte finish tempers the boldness and lends a more stonelike feel, while gloss amps up the drama.

Of course, white is a color, too—and, when it is used correctly, an absence of hue can still leave a colorful impression. The trick is to move beyond plain white ceramic and opt for another material, like glass or marble. For a streamlined look that departs from the norm, consider another format—white mosaic, oversized tiles, or ones with elongated, planklike proportions. Or choose a crackled finish that lends texture without cluttering the room's clean lines. Use white as an excuse to explore the many fabulous relief tiles with sculptural surfaces.

For more options that display the breadth of color choices, see The Options, beginning on page 224.

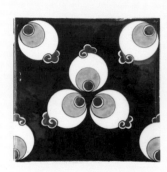

Iznik Tile

Istanbul's awe-inspiring, lushly decorated mosques and palaces reveal the culture's expressionistic use of tiled surfaces—proof that exuberant patterning in eye-popping colors can be remarkably timeless.

Often installed as large wall murals or a scrappy, animated patchwork of different styles, the mesmerizing tiles were produced in the small lakefront town of Iznik, Turkey, some 100 miles away. The region developed a distinctive aesthetic distinguished by swirling scrollwork and florals decorated with a riot of bold colors resembling semiprecious stones like lapis lazuli, turquoise, coral, and emerald. The quartz-based glazes, shiny but not glaring, were also widely believed to have healing properties.

The Iznik masters kept their production methods secret, so when manufacturing died out in the early eighteenth century, the techniques were lost. The art form has recently been revived thanks to research initiated by Istanbul's Iznik Foundation to reproduce the characteristic satiny surface and glasslike feel in the age-old, eco-friendly manner. Reflecting a current vogue for bright colors and animated accent walls, Iznik tiles are gaining popularity once again—reborn as decorative accents and murals in homes across the globe.

Ann Sacks sells many styles of tile in the traditional turquoise, cobalt, and coral palette, all made in Iznik, Turkey, using ancient methods.

1.

WHITE ON WHITE

Above: Interior designers S. Russell Groves and Neal Beckstedt clad a bathroom in elongated 2 by 8-inch tiles of translucent white glass, oriented in a vertical running-bond pattern. *Opposite, above:* The master bathroom is dressed floor to ceiling in Calacatta Oro Gold marble. The designers chose oversized tiles to minimize grout lines and showcase the material's veining. *Opposite, below:* The second bathroom's floor is smoothed over in 12-inch squares of the same Calacatta Oro Gold marble.

A pair of bathrooms in a New York apartment demonstrates the surprising variety one can coax from a white-on-white color scheme. Interior designers S. Russell Groves and Neal Beckstedt deployed a complement of clean creams to instill a sense of lavish calm within both rooms.

For one, the designers envisioned a contemporary riff on old-school subway tile. Instead of glazed white ceramic, they used 2 by 8-inch glass tiles in a warm, milky hue with a hint of translucency. "The material has much more depth than ceramic. We chose one with a little polish so it wouldn't look overly matte," says Beckstedt. The finish gives the walls a glowing quality, like backlit panels—a smart move in a windowless space. The designers ran the material in a vertical staggered-bond pattern to draw attention upward and create the illusion of more headroom. They ended the run of tile a few inches from the ceiling, punctuating it with a polished nickel cap to make it look as if the tile enfolds rather than blankets the room. Twelve-inch squares of crystalline Calacatta Oro Gold marble form the flooring, laid in a sober grid that reins in the liveliness of the walls.

Groves and Beckstedt used the same marble in the master bath. "Like the glass, which is a recycled product, we chose an environmentally friendly material: a locally sourced stone from a Colorado quarry. It's speckled and glittery—a bit like hardened sugar." The sanctuary is clad floor to ceiling in the lavish material—elongated 6 by 24-inch tiles on the wall and oversized 12 by 24-inch rectangles below. The result is a single large wet area, with an open shower and a large soaking tub anchoring one side. "We made the room one big space to showcase the simple grid of beautiful material. Everything else looks like furniture within." Although severe in its articulation—all the grout joints line up rigorously—the spare design is nonetheless warm, a result of choosing natural materials with a soft, welcoming presence and a pleasing, fluid flow of veins and speckles.

Pattern and Shape

In pursuit of pattern? You can thank your lucky stars. The current tile marketplace offers an unprecedented assortment of fashion-forward plaids and houndstooths, roses and tulips, damasks and Greek keys, crocodile and leopard prints. Regardless of your stylistic preferences, there's never been a better time to indulge in animated surface decoration.

Ornamentation can come within the confines of an individual tile that's been printed, painted, etched, glazed, molded, or otherwise embellished. But you can also achieve patterns by mixing plain tiles of various sizes and shapes. Alternating rectangular subway tiles with a row of small mosaics imparts the suggestion of movement, while mixing two hues of 4-inch ceramic squares forms a classic checkerboard. Creative arrangement of solid tiles is the idea behind mosaic art, in which each tile becomes a pixel in an overall composition, be it stripes or paisley or leaves.

Pattern can also manifest itself through the juxtaposition of multiple tiles embellished with graphic motifs that continue from one to another. Cross-hatching, basket weaves, and arabesques that swoosh across the surface of side-by-side tiles delight the eye. Pairing two-dimensional patterning with a surface relief texture heightens the animation; limiting pattern to a tactile treatment is less busy (if no less bold).

Compositional tiles, with designs that stretch across a series of units like a mural, have increased in availability and variety, making designing with pattern a less tricky proposition. Offered in imagery ranging from geometrics to more natural motifs like Japanese-inspired landscapes, you can inset a series of compositionals within a field of the same background color, or overtake an entire wall or floor.

Pattern thus asserts itself through the decoration of the tile, its placement in relationship to other tiles, or even through its shape. Deviate from the grid with hexagons or circles. Choose 1-inch penny mosaics or big circles with ample expanses of contrasting-colored grout in between. With advancements in mold-making, ceramics come in almost any shape, from interlocking fleurs-de-lis to triangles and more abstracted silhouettes reminiscent of barbells. Selecting an unusual shape makes a daring declaration.

A little pattern for an accent wall or a small feature goes a long way, but a more generous expanse can be particularly affecting. Some people shy away from using copious amounts of patterning for fear that it will make a space seem claustrophobic,

1. In her Fire Island home, designer Gail Shields-Miller accented a simple, inexpensive white ceramic tile—installed vertically in a staggered bond pattern—with rows of 1-inch glass mosaics.

2. If you're craving pattern, consider mosaics—either a custom installation designed to your specifications, or an off-the-shelf product providing a bespoke look. These irregularly shaped ceramic tesserae are artfully composed to form an abstracted nature scene.

3. Designer Vanessa Deleon opted for a randomly patterned ceramic mosaic backsplash in a New York apartment.

4. Pattern doesn't require oodles of color for strong impact. In this nook, just alternating gold and marble mosaics—stripes on the walls, a grid on the floor—offers the right hint of liveliness.

Right: For a sense of movement and dynamism, consider deviating from a grid. Installed in a freeform pattern, Ann Sacks's red-and-white glass mosaic invigorates a bathroom. *Opposite:* Caitlin and Samuel Dowe-Sands surfaced a bedroom wall of their historic Marrakech home in coral-patterned cement tiles of their own design, handmade by a local studio using traditional Moroccan manufacturing methods.

but in practice that's not always the case. The effect entirely depends on the unique proportions and character of your space, the tiles you've chosen, and how the tiles are deployed. Indeed, by giving your eye something to bounce across, sometimes decoration actually creates the illusion of more square footage. (This is the reason an empty room often seems much smaller than it does once furnished.) To avoid having the design become too visually active, pick a textured tone-on-tone or one with subtle coloration. When mixing patterns, keep a common element—the palette, dimension, or shape.

If you live with artworks, relegating pattern to the floor—as you would a rug—frees up white space for the walls. Or consider adorning the ceiling, creating pattern with tiles either decorated with imagery or installed in geometric configurations.

For more on pattern and shape, see The Options, pages 275 to 293.

1.

2.

3.

4.

Texture

Many covet tile's inherent surface sleekness, which imparts a modern sensibility—and makes it especially easy to clean. Indeed, those seeking a smooth material treatment for a particular room or nook are likely drawn to tile first. But textured reliefs offer bold decorative possibility while providing another design dimension to play with. Chiseled limestone tiles confer a rustic, lived-in feel and a sense of grandeur. Glazed ceramic molded into geometric patterns confers a dose of midcentury mod. Textured tiles can be quite bold and assertive, but subtler textures invite touch, too. Certain materials like leather or cork have a luxurious natural tactility; use them on the floor, where they will come into most frequent contact with bare skin.

The gamut of wilder textures includes concave and convex, folded and indented, rippled and pyramidal. Ceramic and glass are among the most moldable materials, hence the great variety of textured options within those categories. Relief glass formed into curves or ripples offers the bonus of drawing light into the tile from all sides, like a diamond ring, thus enhancing the surface glow.

Deploy sculptural reliefs where you can best appreciate them—on a fireplace surround, around a window, or in a bathroom to accent a run of a plainer tile. Placement in close proximity to natural illumination emphasizes any surface variegation. Although a little grab underfoot offers protection from slippage, you'll otherwise want to avoid major texture on the floor, where it would be a tripping hazard (most relief tiles are not approved for floor use anyway).

Trendwise, one of the most interesting stories is actually quite subtle: the improved verisimilitude of stonelike porcelains. New scraped finishes that mimic the look of brecchiated (or raked) marbles allow these man-made tiles to pass for the real thing. Subtle dimples and impressions in the surface also help porcelain pass for leather, fabric, wood, and even wallpaper; the unobtrusive texture goes a long way to casting sturdy porcelain in more decorative roles. To explore texture in greater depth, turn to The Options, pages 244 to 253.

1. Tiles of chiseled Jerusalem limestone are typically used for exterior applications, but Nicole Sassaman chose them to conjure a spalike feeling in her shower. She accented the feature walls with expanses of smoother Lagos Azul limestone for the tub surround. **2.** Don't be afraid to use texture in a snug space. It can impart a delightful quality of intimacy, as in this bath. The heavily chiseled limestone is from Artistic Tile.

3. A floor skimmed in 12-inch-square quartzite tiles brings a rustic yet refined charm to a beachside pool house while keeping conditions less slippery underfoot. **4.** Texture isn't always about bold relief patterns and rough stones; a much subtler sense of touch can prove just as effective. Edelman's thin leather strips installed in a parquet pattern have a soft, cosseting feel even in a smoothly polished finish.

Narrowing In

Choosing the right tile for your home demands equal consideration of looks and performance. You fall in love with a certain material—a lushly striated marble, say—and it turns out to be ill suited to the application you had in mind. You adjust by choosing another option with a similar essence but made of tougher stuff. Or you walk into a showroom with a particular set of needs—resistance to heat and mold, for example—and then home in on the tile varieties that best fit the criteria, opting for the one whose appearance you like best. Either way, the selection process inevitably involves weighing form against function.

Consider these points before shopping for tile:

1. LOCATION. Where is the tile going? Walls, floors, fireplaces, wet areas, and wine cellars—each comes with specific criteria for maintenance and installation. Floors must be slip-resistant, shower walls should repel moisture, and fireplace hearths should be both sturdy and fireproof.

2. MAINTENANCE. What intensity and frequency of maintenance can you handle? If you love that marble mosaic but are not up to the task of resealing your floor every year, opt for something else; natural materials generally require continual upkeep.

3. FOIBLES. Be realistic about your foibles. Can you live with a material that changes over time or has variegation, like stone, cork, leather, and even handmade cement? Do unmatched grout joints agitate your inner obsessive-compulsive and drive you a little batty? Address these preferences up front.

4. SPECIAL NEEDS. Do you live in a flood zone? Does your easy-breezy, indoor-outdoor lifestyle mean living with the doors open all the time? Do you have small children who will spend significant amounts of time playing on the floor? Do joint issues make it hard for you to stand for long periods? (In the latter case, more resilient materials will work better.)

Be honest about your own requirements *and* your visual preferences, and don't be shy about communicating them to your designer, supplier, or salesperson.

Size and Format

Right: Oversize formats, such as these 12 by 24-inch tiles from Ann Sacks, are a popular alternative to glass mosaics. The large size enhances the sense of sleekness, unbroken by copious grout lines. *Opposite:* Large squares of limestone cover almost every surface of this tranquil space. When used in wet areas, like this open-plan Florida bathroom, stones should be sealed to resist moisture.

Beyond matters of physical makeup and performance, consider a tile's format. A smaller tile, for instance, is more sensitive to minute flaws or bumps in the substrate and can pop above the surrounding field. And in most cases, larger tiles need a stronger support system.

Meanwhile, a room with lots of nooks and crannies and corners demands a smaller module to wrap around its twists and turns, hence the benefit of penny tile or mosaics. But the smaller the tile size, the more grout joints the surface will have, which affects appearance and performance. Grout tends to dirty, stain, and discolor; in addition, many people find that copious grout lines are busy and make a pint-sized loo seem even smaller. Circumvent this effect by choosing a grout color that matches the tile, creating a more monochromatic field. Also consider a material like gold leaf–backed glass that bounces light around the room or a patterned mosaic whose bold imagery distracts from the grid.

Size is a relative term, of course. The same tile imparts a different sensibility depending on its context. The character and layout of your space will influence your choice of large or small, square or rectangle, circle or hexagon. While conventional wisdom suggests using big tile in a big room and small tile in a small room, any designer will tell you the opposite is often true. A matter of preference and visual perception, size should be considered on a case-by-case basis as one of a complex matrix of interrelated design factors.

1.

2.

3.

4.

Installation Pattern

Pattern also comes into play when choosing tiles. Consider the overall feeling you are trying to achieve. If you find yourself leaning toward surroundings that are sober or modern, pick a stacked pattern with lined-up grout joints. For a more classical look, install tiles in an offset, bricklike fashion called a *running bond*, which is suggestive of movement.

A middle ground is to use a rectangular tile in a stacked pattern. Elongated proportions—2 by 8 inches or 4 by 16—can push the feeling of dynamism to an extreme, as if the tiles themselves are in motion. A rectangular shape also gives you a little more design flexibility, providing the option of running the tiles vertically, which emphasizes ceiling height, or horizontally, which expands the space outward. You can even orient the tiles on the diagonal in a diamond pattern, like herringbone, for more animation.

Mixing patterns along a plane enhances variety, especially when using the same color or size of tile throughout an entire room. Just switching up the top and bottom halves of a wall creates a visual break; deploy a grid of yellow ceramic squares on top and shift to a running bond pattern below. Inset a straight-set floor with an "area rug" of an alternating zigzag pattern, or highlight an architectural feature like a mirror or a column with a change of geometry. Or intermingle three or more sizes of one tile in a meandering, random array. This great trick fools the eye when using stonelike porcelains; the resulting irregular lines make the material look less man-made.

You can also choose between herringbones and basket weaves, dog bones and checks—intricate patterns typically achieved via mosaic or smaller-sized tiles. Patterns can be hand-laid or, more commonly, installed in 12-inch modules held together by a backing of flexible mesh. (In the case of materials like transparent glass, where you'd see straight through the tile to the backing, mosaic modules instead come affixed to a sheet of paper fronting, which is peeled off after installation.) Break from the confines of geometry altogether with a pictorial pattern, like scrolling vines, or a roaring tiger print. While mosaics come in many materials—from coconut to metal—glass, stone, and ceramic offer the greatest breadth of coloration.

1. Mosaics' small size is well suited to innovative installation patterns and wrapping around curved walls—and rendering whimsical graphics.
2. Different shades of aqueous blue glass in a gradient blend bestow a vanity with panache.
3. A mix of green-tinted marble mosaics and glazed ceramics installed in a variety of formats and patterns imparts oh-so-subtle variety.
4. Roca's thin, elongated porcelain tiles could be mistaken for wood planks. Leo Daly mixed three different hues and installed the wall tiles vertically to give this seating area a groovy, outdoorsy look.

The Character of a Space

In addition to these of size, pattern, and shape, there is a factor much harder to put into words: namely, aesthetics. Your choice of material, as well as your preferred installation pattern, should reflect the mood you hope to achieve. Do you aspire to grandeur or more subdued modernism? Do you want your space to have rusticity or refinement? To seem sleek or textured? To be earthy or bold? Every material has a different character.

If you have difficulty determining this on your own, rest assured you're in good company. Many people find it challenging to articulate the finer points of stylistic preferences. Flip through magazines and tear out pages of rooms, colors, or elements you like, then bring this portfolio to your designer or tile showroom to help guide your discussion. Professionals love nothing better than to do their job: to interpret the intangibles and translate them into a coherent, resolved décor.

Above: New York designer Jayne Michaels covered the walls above and below her kitchen cabinetry in mustard-colored glazed ceramics from Heath, installed in a vertical straight-set configuration to draw the eye upward. *Opposite:* Designed by noted mosaic artist Carlo Del Bianco for Bisazza, a pattern of grisaille blossoms set against a metallic-gold background enlivens an entryway.

In a Coconut Grove home, an elaborate steel staircase descends to a floor of colorful vintage cement tiles inlaid with an abstracted floral motif in red and green. The exuberant patterning takes the place of an area rug, which wouldn't hold up as well to the Florida heat and humidity.

Materials

The world of tile offers myriad materials to choose among. Each has a unique character and set of functional limitations as well as a certain degree of both visual and tactile warmth. While a prominently striated marble brings to mind the classic refinement of an Italianate villa, a swath of pebbly river rocks may transport you to a remote Asian resort. Some materials prove quite chameleonlike. Glass, for instance, can seem sleekly modern or soothingly spalike depending on its hue and translucency; embedded with gold leaf, it takes on another quality entirely—one of incredible luxe.

Finish will affect a material's appearance and personality. Leather with a natural brown stain imparts country chic, while one that's been dyed metallic ruby red and embossed with paisley adds a poppier punch. Honed granite offers a quiet, almost meditative presence, while a shinier surface draws out the stone's characteristic exuberance. Within certain categories—ceramics, for instance—you may be faced with a daunting variety of choices, from terra-cotta to white-body earthenware.

Meanwhile, the spectrum of available materials seemingly expands by the day. Here we outline some of the most popular. Although most are illustrated within the context of a room to best convey the personality these materials bring to a space, we've also provided many more examples of individual tiles in the catalog portion of this book, The Options, beginning on page 136. For a deeper understanding of each category, you're encouraged to flip back and forth between sections.

Above: In a New Jersey kitchen, a grid of iridescent recycled-glass mosaics framed in a ropelike border is set into a backsplash of tumbled limestone squares oriented on the diagonal.

Cement and Concrete

Above: A Marrakech courtyard is floored in cement pavers. The material, though strong, is susceptible to water stains. Embrace the patination that arises from wear and tear as part of its charm. *Above right:* Cement tile flooring offers the graphic punch of a bold carpet.

A bedrock of many cultures and countries, from Mexico to Morocco, cement tile is typically enlivened by piquant patterns and abstract shapes. As flooring, these tiles, with their graphic intricacies and hand-finished look, can take on the appearance of painted wood or even luxe wall-to-wall carpeting. Installed on vertical surfaces, a swath of cement can even bestow an exotic, vaguely Arabic ambience.

The tiles, though rather unyielding underfoot, have a warmer feel than many other hard materials and a surprising softness in surface texture. The edges of the patterns are slightly diffused, making them appear hand-painted, a quality that intensifies over time with patination and wear.

The product of painstaking handcraftsmanship, cement tiles are often imported from countries where cottage industry still flourishes. The graphics are composed of differently shaped pieces of cement that fit together like a puzzle. The low-tech manufacturing process dates to the 1800s. First, a craftsman pours varied colors of tinted cement—a mix of sand and mortar, often enhanced with marble powder—into separate compartments of a metal mold similar to a cookie cutter. Once each compartment is filled with cement, the mold is lifted to reveal the multicolored tile. There is often a degree of imperfection, since bits of pigment can mix into neighboring compartments. The pieces are bound together from behind with another layer of cement and placed in a hydraulic press, which applies up to 2 tons of weight. Tiles are then dried and cured in water baths. (Unlike clay, cement does not require heat to cure.)

Concrete tiles are crafted in a similar fashion, either hand-molded or machine-made and air cured. While cement tiles have long offered vibrant patterning, until recently, concrete tiles were typically available in more neutral colors that imparted an industrial chic. Lately, though, artisans and designers have been experimenting with bolder colors, intriguing hexagonal shapes, and imprinted surfaces with more decorative punch.

PROS

- Cement and concrete tiles are inherently eco-friendly, composed of natural ingredients and often handmade.
- Both materials have a beautiful, almost chalky hand-drawn look that works well in traditional and modern spaces alike.
- Their sturdy surfaces hold up well to the elements and can be used out of doors in temperate areas.
- These dense tiles pair well with radiant heat. A staple of warm climates, they offer coolness underfoot yet visual warmth.

CONSIDERATIONS

- Cement and concrete are sturdy materials, but the surface does develop a patina as the tiles are walked on.
- While they can be used indoors and out, given suitable climate and installation considerations, the material's porosity makes it vulnerable to stains. Only frost-rated tiles should be used outside, and they should be properly sealed.
- Surface treatments can vary from glossy finishes to sandier, matte ones, depending on the desired look.

NUTS AND BOLTS

- **Installation.** Lay over a strong substrate such as concrete or plywood and adhere with thinset mortar.
- **Maintenance.** Protect cement tiles with a chemical sealant or a coat of carnauba wax to add luster, and be prepared to embrace the material's lovely patina. Both cement and concrete can be swept or mopped with a mild cleanser.

For dozens more cement and concrete tiles, see The Options, pages 138 to 139.

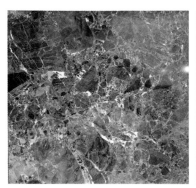

Granite   Slate   Soapstone

Types of Stone

A mind-boggling amount of stones exist. Chuck Muehlbauer, the technical director of the Marble Institute of America, estimates that there are some six thousand types of raw stone on the American market alone. Thus it's important to do your homework and choose the right stone for the right application. Some, like granite, perform universally well under tough conditions—from fireplaces to fountains—while others, including snow white Thassos, are often better suited to decorative applications such as feature walls. A few popular options, in a nutshell:

Granite is one of the hardest and least porous stones. It can withstand frost and freezing and resists the scuffs and scratches of constant traffic (as well as the damaging tread of salty winter boots). Igneous stones, like granite and quartz, are the best choice for a kitchen because they do not react to acids and chemicals. But some find them extremely hard and cold underfoot and unforgiving on dropped items. Staining may also result if they are improperly sealed.

A tough stone, **slate** resists stains, scratches, and water and features a distinctive, irregular cleft surface that provides great traction. (You can get it in a smoother honed finish, too.) The material comes in a variety of colors from graphite to almost orange. Rough, cleft-textured slates can feel quite warm and less sleek than other stones, and darker colors hold sunlight well.

Soapstone, a favorite of high-school chemist labs, is a low-maintenance option

Marble **Limestone** **Quartzite** **Travertine**

that's nonporous and resistant to acids. It also holds heat and releases it slowly over time, so it pairs exceptionally well with radiant systems.

Porous and soft, **marble** wears beautifully. It's a little more soothing underfoot than other stones and has a luminescent quality as well as veining that ranges from striped to spidery. Moreover, marble is offered in seemingly every color of the rainbow, from brilliant red to sultry, speckled green. Since it is composed of calcite, though, it is affected by acids like lemon juice, vinegar, and soda.

Limestone, like marble, performs very well outdoors but is more vulnerable in the kitchen, where it can be damaged by acids like lemon juice. Both stones also stain easily—proceed with caution, red wine drinkers!—and can get scuffed and scratched by sharp objects. Limestone's signature creamy beauty makes it a favorite for spaces ranging from historic to modern. Visual warmth goes hand in hand with a coziness underfoot.

Quartzite is a kind of sandstone that's hard and weather resistant. Thus it is a great option for pools and other high-traffic areas. Some varieties impart rusticity, while others can look quite sophisticated and refined. The dense stone works nicely with radiant heat.

Travertine has a buttery, mellow character reminiscent of Tuscan homes and ancient churches. Available in a range of soft beiges and browns, it has a cosseting quality to the touch. Travertine has a distinctive pockmarked surface that can be left alone or filled with unsanded grout or polyester filler to give it a smoother look and feel. Nonetheless, it is subject to staining and affected by acids, so it requires proper care and sealing.

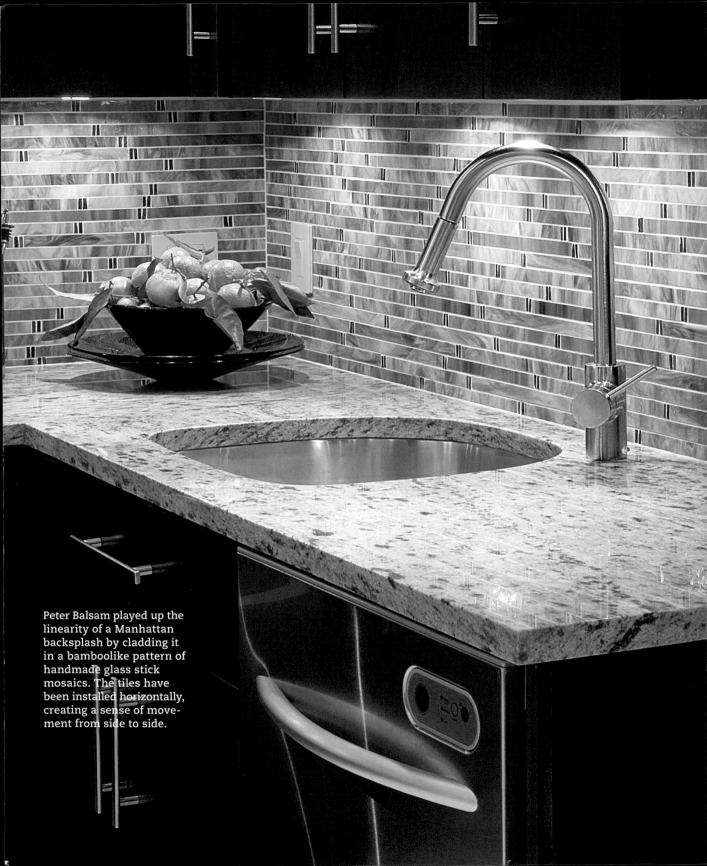

Peter Balsam played up the linearity of a Manhattan backsplash by cladding it in a bamboolike pattern of handmade glass stick mosaics. The tiles have been installed horizontally, creating a sense of movement from side to side.

PROS

- Stone has a beautiful natural character and wears well over time.
- Some types, like granite and slate, are among the sturdier surfacing materials.
- A vast variety of looks and finishes is available.

CONSIDERATIONS

- Many stones can be damaged by acids, so pick carefully when designing a kitchen.
- A natural product, stone's material makeup is never uniform. Even stone sourced from the same quarry can vary wildly. Thus, it's always recommended to get the most current sample from your showroom before making a final selection.
- Stone is porous, and many varieties can discolor and scratch. This doesn't mean you should rule out limestone for your kitchen floor; it *does* mean you should consider how you feel about surface flaws and whether an imperfect, evolving patina is right for you.
- Even when properly sealed, many kinds of stone still absorb minerals from water and dull over time.
- Always do thorough research when purchasing natural stone. The product's performance depends on its composition and inherent characteristics as well as the finish, application, and how carefully it's installed.

NUTS AND BOLTS

- **Installation.** Lay over a level substrate and adhere with thinset mortar. Some types of green marble may curl at the edges if backed with a water-based mortar, in which case a silicone adhesive is preferred.
- **Finish.** Finishes greatly affect a stone's performance and character; granite polished to a reflective gloss is wild and animated, while a honed finish develops a subdued matrix of diodes and flecks. Illumination bounces off a polished surface and penetrates a honed one; thus, polished finishes draw out patterns, while honed finishes mute them. Polished finishes are better designed to ward off red wine and lemon juice, and they are easier to clean, too. But they can be slippery and show scratches. Honed finishes have more traction but are also more absorbent and thus prone to staining. Outdoors, steer toward flamed or cleft-faced finishes, which maximize surface texture in order to minimize slips. The finish dictates the type of sealant to apply.
- **Sealant.** Stones should be sealed about once a year—more often in high-traffic areas and less often in decorative applications. If a particularly impervious stone, like granite, is installed for decorative effect only or in an area with light traffic, a sealant may not be required at all. Consult your supplier for a professional recommendation.
- **Enhancer.** Many stones require one or more coats of enhancer to draw out the full intensity of their natural patterning. Test samples prior to installation.
- **Maintenance.** Stone's durability depends on proper maintenance. Unlike composites and porcelains, stone has not been engineered to resist the elements, be they your children or the weather. Clean regularly with neutral, nonacid solutions.

To acquaint yourself with the vast world of natural stones, turn to The Options, pages 140 to 148.

Leather

Leather's use as a treatment for walls and floor dates back to the cave dwellers. More recently, architect Philip Johnson famously (and daringly) used leather flooring in his Glass House, while 1940s French designer Jean-Michel Frank favored the material for a number of residential interiors. But enhanced coatings, novel installation systems, and an explosion in color palette have made leather a much more varied category, bringing the venerable material squarely into the twenty-first century. With higher-quality finishes, even hair-on hides are more resistant to water, stains, and fading. Today, you can also find products with magnetized backing that stick to metallized walls and floors, making leather tiles easy to swap out seasonally or if one gets damaged or worn.

This is no small consideration, since living materials have natural variation and patinate with wear, taking on a personality of their own. If you appreciate how stone develops character over time, leather might be a good material for you. But be prepared to accept that it *will* weather and age. Direct sun, scuffing, and even wine can affect it. Avoid leather if you're lusting after a meticulous, spotless, and even-tempered surface.

Superficial aging aside, leather is surprisingly durable. High-quality leather wears *in,* not out. Think of an old saddle, your well-loved club chair, or a vintage Hermès handbag. If cared for properly, it should last for many years. Leather's elegance and softness make it seem much more delicate than it is—don't forget that it once protected an animal out in the wild.

Many leather tiles are a by-product of the food industry. Once the cow's meat is removed, the hides are repurposed for decorative applications. The tiles originate from the toughest, thickest part of the hides: right along the spine. (Only the strongest fibers are suited to floor tiles.) Like any hides, those used to make tiles have to be brought back to life. The tanning process rejuvenates the leather, giving it the supple texture and aroma for which it is coveted. Purists prefer tile leather tanned the old-fashioned way, with natural vegetable oils derived from tree bark—a combination of old-school values and nouveau chic.

Above: **Richly textured leather tiles from Edelman enliven a dining vignette. A buttery hue skims the walls, where the leather is subjected to less wear and tear, while the floors are smoothed over in lush brown 12-inch squares inset with 4-inch-square black accents.**

PROS

- Compared to stone and ceramic, leather is incredibly supple, offering a sense of warmth. Less assertive brown and chocolate hues look almost like wood floors but are much softer to the touch.

- Its tactility is especially appreciable in small spaces like a closet, an elevator cab, or a powder room.

- Leather is tailor-made for areas like the bedroom or a media room, where it can also absorb sound and improve acoustics.

- In snug quarters or where installed over radiant heat, leather emits a more intense aroma.

- It ages well and develops a beautiful patina if properly cared for.

CONSIDERATIONS

- Leather is a living material that will wear over time—that's part of its charm. The first scratch or ding will likely cause some alarm, though.

- High-quality products offer the best bet for standing up to wear and tear. You'll want the most pristine leather tiles from exceptionally clean hides, free of scars and with a full, unadulterated grain. Be wary of the cheaper stuff made from imperfect hides, smoothed over with a sanding wheel and stamped with an artificial grain. These don't have the natural resilience of the more upscale versions.

- Hides should be dyed all the way through to ensure that the color remains the same over the course of natural wear.

- Because they are dyed in lots, there is often a slight variation in color from tile to tile. Prefer a more uniform look? Gravitate to darker colors or denser patterns.

- Leather and water do not mix. Powder room walls are fair game, but avoid using leather where it will be subjected to more than the occasional splash. Leather tiles are not the ideal choice for kitchens or master baths. Only those treated with specialized coatings are appropriate for high-traffic or wet areas.

- Salt, even saltwater, will ruin the finish, so save leather for your country cottage, not your beach house.

NUTS AND BOLTS

- **Preinstallation.** As a living material, leather needs time to acclimate to its environment—at least 48 hours, or more depending on humidity level.

- **Installation.** Leather should be installed by a contractor experienced in working with the material. Lay over a level and even plywood subfloor, which has a bit of flex, allowing the resilient material to breathe and shift. The adhesive used to glue down leather will pop the paper finish off Sheetrock, so wall tiles should always be laid over plywood instead.

- **Finish.** Tiles should be sealed after installation and waxed and buffed periodically thereafter—several times a year, depending on traffic. (When the tiles start to look dull rather than delicious, you know it's time; be careful not to overdo it, though, because they can get slippery.) Floors should be waxed and buffed three times prior to walking on them.

- **Cleaning.** Dust occasionally with a dry mop or cloth, as you would hardwood flooring.

For dozens more leather options, see The Options, pages 150 to 153.

Right: A backsplash is an ideal place to use wood, since tiles will be subject to minimal moisture and splashing. This kitchen is clad in Fortis Arbor sustainable solid-teak mosaics, handmade by Flux Studios.

Wood

While rich, velvety walnut and light-stained oak are typically installed as elongated planks, today's marketplace offers a full complement of wood tiles, too. Many people lump parquet and end-grain—thinly sliced cross sections of square beams—into the hardwood flooring category, but both can be considered tile, available in modular formats that are glued to a subfloor.

Parquet comes in a mélange of styles and patterns, from zigzag herringbones and starched-and-pressed checks to elaborate motifs that simulate inlay. Think of parquet as a mosaic of small wood shapes, pieced together and placed on a backing to form squares. Tiles click together in a tongue-and-groove fashion and then are glued down. (The same process applies to engineered wood and laminates, which occasionally fall into the wood tile category, too.)

Durability distinguishes end-grain, often used for factory floors, where its strength is prized. But its textured, rough-hewn appearance looks just as compelling in spaces ranging from modern-industrial lofts to more rustic, ethnic homes.

Intriguing new formats like wood mosaics have elevated this age-old building material into an innovative product with a whole new character. Choose between squares, hexes, diamond shapes with a slight pillowed surface texture, and 1-inch mosaics pieced together to showcase their variety of color and grain. Many are created from leftover scrap wood used to make other products and are thus an environmentally friendly option, too.

If you seek something with a little more intrigue and exoticism than the expected walnut, oak, and pine, peruse all the wood varieties at your disposal, including teak and rosewood. You can also obtain sustainable materials like bamboo and even mesquite. Distinguished by a warm reddish-brown hue, mesquite is dense and fast-growing; manufacturer Ann Sacks, for one, crafts it into beautiful tiles that can be installed on walls in various thicknesses for a textured relief.

PROS

- Wood imparts a warm, rich, and lustrous look.
- On floors, the tiles can approximate hardwood planks.
- An array of styles is available, from parquet to mosaics.
- Wood is much warmer underfoot and to the touch than harder surfaces like stone or ceramic.

CONSIDERATIONS

- Like wood floorboards, wood tiles are generally suited to dry areas only.
- A natural product, wood fades with exposure to sunlight over time unless treated to a UV-protectant coating.
- Many high-end tile showrooms offer a range of wood products such as mosaics. For parquet and engineered woods, you may have to seek out suppliers who specialize in the material or sell hardwood flooring, into which category these products typically fall.

NUTS AND BOLTS

- **Preinstallation.** Wood tiles should be adjusted to the humidity level of their surroundings, ideally for at least 48 hours.
- **Installation.** Lay on a level plywood or concrete subfloor using a gluelike mastic adhesive rather than mortar.
- **Finish.** Manufacturers often recommend that, when used on floors, wood tiles be finished and sealed. Many can be lightly sanded and refinished as they show signs of wear.
- **Maintenance.** A rose by any other name is still a rose. Treat your wood tile as you would hardwood planks: Wipe up spills quickly, vacuum to clean, and avoid harsh cleaning agents.

To discover the full bounty of wood tiles, turn to The Options, pages 154 to 155.

Right: In their L.A. kitchen, Jim and Nancy Chuda installed cork flooring for its environmental friendliness. The tiles soften acoustics, while the bold speckled pattern hides both wear and stains.

Cork

Put a cork in it? Yes indeed—especially if you're on the hunt for a tile that is soft underfoot yet still incredibly durable. Cork is a high-performance option, one with a welcoming natural beauty and a slight sense of quirk.

Although a popular choice for homes and even high-traffic public spaces in the early twentieth century—modernist architects Joseph Eichler and Frank Lloyd Wright were big fans—cork fell out of favor in the postwar era, replaced by cheaper resilients like vinyl and linoleum. But recent years have seen a flood of exciting new products that showcase cork's chameleonlike character. Yes, there are still earth-toned square-format tiles in a soothing range of browns and beiges—the source of the material's somewhat crunchy connotations. Now, though, you can also find blue-tinted cork planks that mimic painted floorboards, cork mosaics with a fun and poppy feel, and unusual geometric shapes like zigzags and hexagonals. Paler versions installed in rectangular formats can even mimic stone. And easy-to-install temporary versions, perfect for reviving an old vinyl floor, are also available.

Courtesy of its earthy good looks, cork is often considered the stuff of tree-huggers. And, indeed, it is all-natural and environmentally friendly, a product of the Mediterranean cork oak tree. Throughout the trees' long life spans, their relatively fast-growing bark is trimmed—like a haircut—every nine years. The granular bark is then pressed into molds and baked; the longer heat is applied, the darker the resulting color.

Cork has a suppleness that's easy on the joints. The material has a cellular structure that encompasses thousands of minute air bubbles, not unlike a sponge. You can't see the little cells with the naked eye, but you can feel them with your feet. Walk across a cork floor and you immediately note its springiness. For this reason, it's a wonderful choice for kids' rooms or play areas in which small children (and their parents) spend lots of time on the floor. If the hardness of ceramic and porcelain has made you steer clear of a tile-floored kitchen in the past, consider cork as an alternative. A bonus for the klutzy and fumble-fingered: cushiony cork is particularly forgiving on glassware and china that's slipped out of wet hands.

Above: **Because cork absorbs noise, it's a smart choice for work-intensive home offices. Here, cork tiles in a pale, almost white hue look like a sleeker material altogether.**

Metal

Metal tiles are often used as sculptural decorative inserts, slipped at regular intervals into a contrasting swath of stone or tile. The shiny finish lends brightness, sparking a more matte material surrounding it and accenting it like jewelry. Akin to natural stone, metal finishes tend to patinate with age to take on a softly burnished look—an expression of their living character.

Above: **Tough enough to withstand foot traffic, a grid of 12-inch-square recycled aluminum pavers welcomes visitors to a Los Angeles home. The surface takes on a lovely patina over time, building up little scratches with wear— a living finish.**

Inserts come in various materials and finishes, including copper and gold. Each has its own distinct character, with stainless steel looking the most slickly modern and white bronze among the most traditional and luxe. Some insets are quite detailed, with heavily carved reliefs in florets; others feature more abstract motifs—evidence of metal's incredible flexibility as a decorative accent.

Metal is also gaining prominence as a full-blown wall and floor covering. Large squares of patinated aluminum bring shine to a space, while stainless-steel mosaics in the shape of water-worn river rocks offer an unexpected touch for a powder room. While many think metal tiles, particularly in large quantities, can read as cold or overly sleek, that's nothing more than a cliché. Given the spectrum of finishes, shapes, and sizes that metal comes in, the material can impart a velvety or suedelike impression. A rougher, more organic surface treatment can soften the look and temper the shine, while a hammered texture confers a handmade quality.

Although the material's softer side is big news today, many still prefer to play up its hard-edge quality. If you are one, then opt for stainless steel. The finish is durable and the look extremely exact and almost precision-engineered. Another choice is aluminum tile, which has a bright and silvery personality. Long used in the construction and aerospace industries, aluminum is lightweight and malleable yet incredibly strong. Its reflective, mirrored surface can open up small rooms, creating an illusion of expansiveness.

Eco-friendly aluminum can be repeatedly recycled without losing any of its structural integrity. A few boutique companies capitalize on this capability with tiles formed from recycled soda cans and other scraps. The difference between recycled and virgin aluminum is one of look; recycled aluminum often features tiny air bubbles that add texture, depth, and character to the surface—bringing the medium happily full circle to its artisanal origins.

PROS

- Metal tiles come in sizes ranging from small decorative accent pieces and penny-tile mosaics to larger-format squares and rectangles.
- A spectrum of finishes and materials—including stainless steel, bronze, and aluminum—is available to suit almost any look.
- Tough aluminum tiles are ideal for exterior applications where they can outlast asphalt.
- Metal tiles are generally thin and quite dense, and thus pair well with radiant flooring.

CONSIDERATIONS

- Foot traffic scratches and dulls the surface metal over time. While this lends a beautiful luster and patina, the first ding can be alarming. Some like a living patina; some don't.
- Know what you're getting. Some tiles are metal through and through, while less expensive versions generally bond a metal veneer to a ceramic backing. While many of the latter prove quite tough, they are less so than a tile composed entirely of the same content.
- Courtesy of its sleekness, metal tiles are often perceived as colder than many other surfaces. This is incorrect, as metal, like other materials, actually takes on the temperature of the surrounding room. Nonetheless, it tends to feel slicker underfoot than wood, leather, and even many ceramics.

NUTS AND BOLTS

- **Installation.** Metal tiles are installed like any other kind, with thinset or a mortar bed. Stainless steel, though, requires a framework to contain the tiled area, since the tile edges are not always refined. Stainless-steel tiles work for floor applications as well as on walls and ceilings, as long as you have a strong substrate and fasteners to provide extra holding power.
- **Finish.** Aluminum oxidizes if improperly sealed. It can be painted or spray-finished. A greener option is an integral powder coat, applied by running a current through the metal at a high temperature.
- **Cleaning.** Most metal tiles can be cleaned with mild detergent.
- **Maintenance.** Decorative metal insets can be left to patinate or shined and buffed to restore their luster. You can use steel wool, but be careful not to abrade any sensitive surrounding surfaces, like natural stone.

To view additional metal tiles, turn to The Options, pages 156 to 163.

Glass is a particularly varied material, available in many colors, degrees of opacity, and shapes. Artistic Tile makes these glam silver leaf–backed versions, whose sinuous form suggests falling leaves.

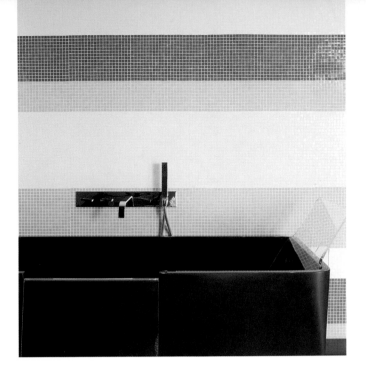

Glass

The most distinctive characteristic of glass is its luminosity, dancing light and sparkle around the room. It can seem almost immaterial, more a window to some mystical space beyond than a flat surface. A conduit for color, glass injects vibrancy and joie de vivre. Its lustrous sheen bestows a pristine quality to a space. It looks clean without being cold, rich and luxurious but still lighthearted.

The signature durability of glass defies its delicate, often gemlike appearance; mosaic has long been used to clad building exteriors, where it proves a formidable foil to the elements. While its heat resistance and imperviousness to water and chemicals have historically made it a popular finish in wet areas like bathrooms and kitchens, lately glass has moved from the sidelines to a starring role in other areas of the home, too—as an unexpected flooring option in a master suite or on a dining room accent wall.

The rising popularity of patterned mosaics has spurred renewed interest in the material—and a demand for a broader range of formats. Glass is a flexible option, now readily available in myriad looks and styles. One-inch-square mosaics in continuous or blended shades might still be the category's best sellers, but you can also choose between opaque and transparent material, saturated hues and more restful colors, or tiles that have been backpainted or embedded with intoxicating gold leaf. Larger sizes—up to 12 by 24 inches—are flooding the market, too, as well as 4 by 16-inch and even 1 by 12-inch tiles.

Above left: Glass is a delightful conduit for color. Trend's chromatic mosaics are a sharp touch behind a dark soaking tub, bringing a jolt of energy to bathing time.

PROS

- The glossy finish enhances illumination.
- Impervious to water, chemicals, and stains, its shiny surface makes glass easy to keep clean of mildew and dirt.
- Providing unlimited creative freedom, glass comes in a vast assortment of colors, finishes, patterns, and textures as well as sizes ranging from small mosaics to large formats.
- The material's sense of depth makes a room seem more expansive.

CONSIDERATIONS

- Glass can crack if not properly laid, so find an expert installer with a gentle touch, one who's well versed in the material.
- Mosaics can be painstaking to apply; many come affixed to sheets of paper fronting that must be wet with a sponge and peeled off after installation. This means a lengthier installation process, a higher risk of flaws, greater cost, and the need for a highly experienced contractor.
- Even the most opaque glass still has some degree of translucency. Thus, using white thinset is the best way to guarantee that the color, once installed, is exactly what you ordered. Even a subtle gray tint behind back-painted glass affects its surface coloration.

NUTS AND BOLTS

- **Installation.** Glass is not the easiest material to apply to walls and floors, especially in the ever-popular mosaic format. Its prized translucency is a bête noire for installers; unless the tile is back-painted or metal-leafed, you can see right through to the wall behind. It's important to use a white mortar that's less visible, and see-through tiles must also be back-buttered (that is, their back sides skimmed with another layer of mortar), since there is no place for flaws like air bubbles and lumps to hide. Because of this, the installation process can be slow and painstaking.
- **Cracking.** Cracked glass is usually a result of a subpar installation. To prevent movement and fissures, most manufacturers recommend a fracture membrane—a sheet of rubber or latex applied over the substrate and below the tiles—coupled with fastidious caulking and ample expansion joints.
- **Grout.** Most installers use unsanded grout to avoid abrading the shiny surface. A nice effect for walls is to fill the joints just three-quarters of the way—deep enough to hold the tiles in place but shallow enough to let a little light pass through the side of the tile and create enhanced illumination.
- **Maintenance.** Use a glass cleaner like Windex or water mixed with ammonia.

Turn to The Options, pages 164 to 171 to acquaint yourself with the full spectrum of glass tiles.

Opposite: **For a little bling, consider crystal inserts. A curved shower enclosure bedecked in shades of pink mosaic from Trend is inset with shimmering Swarovski gems.**

PROS

- Porcelain is generally impervious to water, mold, mildew, scratching, chipping, and breaking.

- Styles run the gamut from tiles reminiscent of limestone and other natural materials to those with design-forward fashion prints.

- Many manufacturers now offer greener porcelains with higher recycled content. Some even come impregnated with purifiers that clean the surrounding air, removing dust and allergens.

- Ideal for wet areas, porcelain comes in slip-resistant finishes that perform well yet are imperceptible to the eye.

- It holds heat well and stays cool in the summer, so it is good for keeping energy costs down. It also pairs nicely with radiant heat.

- Plainer versions can be quite affordable compared to other specialty materials.

CONSIDERATIONS

- The toughest porcelains are "through-body," with color and patterning that extends from top to bottom, thus disguising surface wear. Glazed versions are tough underneath, but the surface can still scratch; ultimately, porcelains are only as strong as their finish, and some high-design versions should be used only on walls.

- One of the best things about porcelain is how enduring and long-lasting it is. But if you are tempted to indulge in a particularly trendy, decorative style, keep in mind that tile is not as changeable as wallpaper if you outgrow it.

- Because it is so hard and dense, porcelain can be tough on knees and joints in places like kitchens where you stand for long periods.

NUTS AND BOLTS

- **Installation.** Porcelain tiles are ideally laid over a solid substrate, like plywood or concrete, with a thinset mortar. However, new versions backed in fiberglass mesh can be installed directly over existing tiles. Innovative systems combining tile and substrate into one easy-to-install package are available.

- **Format.** Some oversized porcelains are now thin enough for walls, too. Still, large formats are not ideal for wobblier, older construction.

- **Grout versus no grout.** Rectified porcelains with smoothed-over edges can be installed without grout. However, many experts recommend against rectified installations in places subjected to significant movement, like high-traffic floors or walls surrounding a constantly slamming door; with no grout to stabilize shockwaves, the tiles can lift up a few millimeters and compromise the integrity of the surface.

- **Maintenance.** Perhaps the most low-maintenance of tiles, porcelain can be cleaned with any agent. Still, avoid abrasives that affect glazes or grout.

Witness porcelain's wide aesthetic variety in The Options, pages 201 to 211.

True or Faux

If you think porcelain is beige and blah, you are in for an exciting surprise.

Courtesy of technological advancements in mold-making and printing techniques, porcelain tiles can take on the look of almost any other material, from stone and wood to leather and bamboo. If you've always wanted grass cloth or wallpaper in your shower, here's your chance. These porcelain surfaces are ideal for high-traffic areas, working kitchens prone to spills, and wet areas, too. Porcelain can mimic . . .

woven leather

natural stone

lace

wallpaper

sheet metal

fabric

terra-cotta

leather

wood planks

woven-metal textiles

wood mosaics

button-tufted
upholstered panels

horn

bamboo shades

painted wood

silk toile

1.

2.

3.

4.

Going Green

If environmental friendliness is your top priority, there are many ways to go green—from tiles made from sustainable materials to ones incorporating recycled content. Think carefully about a product's composition as well as how and where it's manufactured. A material formed from all-organic resources that's been shipped halfway around the world may not be as green a choice as a product made locally using a smaller percentage of eco-friendly ingredients. And while you might think stone is about as natural as you can get, since it's plucked straight from the earth, the quarrying process itself can have a negative impact on the environment.

Tile's durability allows it to live forever in a space—a boon in light of today's feverish embrace of environmentally friendly building practices. Most discussions of green design focus on home furnishing and building products made from sustainable or recyclable materials. But overlooked in the hype is that the greenest thing you can do is either keep what's already there or use materials that will never need replacing because of wear or outdated styling. Many varieties of tile, from buttery limestone to modernist glazed ceramics, promise such structural and stylistic longevity.

Luckily, tile is an inherently green choice no matter how you cut it. Its modular format means it can be replaced in pieces rather than wholesale in the event of any damage; if a tile chips, you needn't rip up the whole wall. Tiled surfaces also have a positive impact on indoor air quality. Hard materials are easier to clean and don't harbor allergens. Breathe easy by keeping these additional pointers in mind:

1. Leave well enough alone. If you already have tile in your home, the greenest thing you can do is recycle it—that is, leave it there. Learn to love it as is, even if it's not your style. Embrace its quirk, plan your décor to downplay its presence, or freshen it with a porcelain coat or new grout. Natural stones can even be refinished, which gives certain varieties a whole new look. Consider this route before buying a new floor and placing your old one in a landfill.

1. Flux Studios' Fortis Arbor mosaics are handcrafted from scraps of solid hardwoods like teak and bamboo salvaged from furniture makers' studios. **2.** In a bath off Nancy and Jim Chuda's kitchen, 1-inch recycled glass mosaics in brilliant ruby red drench all four walls, including the walk-in shower. The mesmerizing hue is softened by the material's translucent quality, which brings depth and dimension to the space. **3.** In their effort to make their Los Angeles home as green as possible, the Chudas used eco-friendly finishes from top to bottom. In a guest bathroom, a colorful mosaic of recycled-content glass spruces up the walls of a shower, which is floored in recycled aluminum. **4.** Cork, like the tiles flooring this Montauk wine cellar, is a sustainably farmed, all-natural material that also repels dust mites and other allergens.

2. SOURCE LOCALLY. To minimize the waste of fossil fuels, tree-huggers advocate buying as many furnishings and building products as possible within five hundred miles of your home. This may limit you to American manufacturers or overseas labels with localized U.S. production. Save gas by purchasing stones quarried in the United States, like New England slate or Colorado marble, rather than stones imported from Europe or South America.

3. RECYCLE. Reclaimed stones salvaged from old churches, 1920s Belgian cement pavers, vintage American vitrolite—these are just a few of the preowned options available to you. Using tiles that once graced another person's home diverts product from landfill. But, as described above, it can also entail shipping across the globe. Source salvage from as close to home as possible.

4. SEEK OUT RESPONSIBLE MAKERS. These days, many manufacturers—from small studios to large labels—embrace sustainable practices that address factory air quality and minimize the waste of raw materials. Ask your showroom to point out such collections. If your salesperson doesn't have all the answers about a tile's degree of eco-friendliness, dig into the manufacturer's literature or website—or just call and ask about its environmental stance. It's worth taking this extra step to ensure getting a product made in a responsible, ethical manner.

5. PICK SUSTAINABLE MATERIALS. Choose tiles made from things like bamboo and cork that are quickly renewed. Many great options repurpose waste material from other industries—including leather, coconut, glass, terrazzo, engineered stones, and ceramics made of recycled content. ("Post-industrial" recycled content was salvaged from the factory floor; "post-consumer" was diverted from a landfill.) Most manufacturers that make the effort to use sustainable or recycled ingredients embrace green manufacturing, too—but not always. Also, the inclusion of some recycled content doesn't automatically preclude the possibility that something more toxic, like resin, is also mixed in. Ask the tough questions.

6. GO FOR A WARM GLOW FROM BELOW. Radiant subfloor heating creates better indoor air quality than forced air systems because dust particles and microbes aren't blown around. It can also prove a more efficient and economic way to warm your home, since heat is applied directly to your body.

7. SEAL THE DEAL. Keep your tile and stone looking like new—and keep volatile chemicals out of the air—by opting for one of the myriad water-based and VOC-free finishes and sealers. Your showroom or manufacturer can often recommend one appropriate for your product.

8. DO YOUR RESEARCH. Contact the U.S. Green Building Council (see Resources, page 313) for tips and resources about the intricacies of your decisions.

Old World Versus Newly Aged

If natural stone is prized for its unique coloration and veining, salvaged antique surfaces go one step further—coveted not only for their aesthetic beauty but for rarity and provenance, too.

Think of artisanal hand-cut French limestone rescued from a crumbling château or smoky blue cement pavers found in Belgium. Reclaimed stones have a beautifully worn patina unattainable by faux aging. Stains, chipped edges, and other imperfections contribute to their singular beauty. Moreover, an antique stone's age is a testament to its durability.

Two drawbacks accompany reclaimed products. Because many varieties of ancient stones are no longer quarried, they can be prohibitively expensive. (Even expert restorers tend to use reclaimed material only when they require a perfect geological match.) Secondly, limited quantities make it difficult to accommodate larger installations. It can pay to think on a small scale.

Elegant patinas and exotic origins aside, reclaimed stone provides a great way to go green. In effect, you're recycling. Salvaged materials are one of the most environmentally sound ways to build. Of course, there is a trade-off: the cost of fossil fuels to ship reclaimed product across the globe versus the environmental impact of quarrying. If eco-friendliness concerns you, seek out reclaimed stones sourced locally.

Regardless of where your stone comes from—a New England church or an Italian villa—stick to a reputable retailer. Quality depends on the talent, knowledge, and thoroughness of those who find and salvage the material. Stones should be carefully inspected for contamination, moisture, and mold and then properly sealed. Prior exposure to weather, salt, and chemicals can greatly affect a stone's performance in your home.

A combination of budget, project size, and product availability determines whether reclaimed stone tiles are a good fit for you. If you aspire to an Old-World European décor but aren't keen on the high cost of achieving it, you're in luck. A practical alternative is new stones that have been artificially distressed by hand or machine, a technology that continues to improve and output incredibly realistic facsimiles. While they may not have a backstory as intriguing as that of a limestone pulled from a rural English castle, they can certainly look the part.

Artistic Tile's 12-inch squares of hand-chiseled antiqued Bianca Carrera marble inset with swaths of complementary mosaics lend Old-World charm to a foyer.

The Little Details

You've had the chance to mull where you might use tile, what kind of atmosphere you hope to create with it, and the many materials available to help fulfill your vision. The next step entails acquainting yourself with certain design tools to compose two-dimensional surfaces—and three-dimensional spaces. For tile is not just a material but also a module, one that gets arranged in various configurations. Understanding the purpose of specialized trim pieces and the aesthetic implications of grout will help you achieve a well-thought-out installation. Certain challenges—from wet-space considerations to gravity—may affect your plans as well, and further winnow your choices.

Opposite: Vanessa Deleon blanketed the walk-in shower of a New York apartment in floor-to-ceiling white-marble mosaics. She lined the back wall's niches in the same 17 by 26-inch damask-print porcelain used to clad the vanity area a few feet away.

The Elements of Tile: From Bullnoses to V-Caps

A visit to any stone and tile showroom reveals a vast assortment of differently (and sometimes peculiarly) shaped and sized tiles, many with rather compelling, sinuous forms. If you've always envisioned tile as flat and square, you are in for quite a surprise. In addition to square and rectangular tiles, you'll find round tiles and hexagonal tiles, big tiles and small tiles, X-shaped tiles and V-shaped tiles. You'll discover tiles with one glazed or curved edge to wrap around corners, and tiles that look too impossibly small and jewelry-like to be considered tile at all.

Don't be alarmed. Despite all the fancy names—bullnoses and V-caps, listellos and keys—tiles basically fall into three categories: field tile, accents, and trim pieces.

Field Tile

First and perhaps most important is field tile, which covers a swath of wall, floor, ceiling, or any other continuous surface. These aren't just installed in large expanses; you can use field tiles to clad the surfaces of nooks and windowsills and backsplashes, too. Because field tiles are installed next to one another, they do not have smoothed or glazed edges; the rougher surface makes grout adhere better.

Accents

Accent pieces are set into the field tile to add variety and pizzazz. Accents can highlight the color, finish, or geometry of the field tile or inject a little distinctive sparkle and magic. Accent tiles can be interspersed at regular intervals to break up the monotony of a generous expanse of field tile or used to draw borders, lines, boxes, or friezes within surfaces of any size or dimension.

An accent should enhance your field tile, not jar the eye or otherwise compete with the main event. The materials should be complementary, whether in color palette or simply in essence. Tiles of contrasting colors or finish can work together provided there is some commonality of tone or character; metal and stone could not be more different in feel but can be quite close in texture, for instance. A stainless-steel key inset into a quartzite field tile is lovely indeed, drawing out the silvery undertones in both.

The accent tile category includes various specialty tiles:

- **Liners** and **listellos.** Long, narrow pieces used to form stripes or borders.
- **Inserts.** Smaller tiles, often in unusual materials like metal, mother-of-pearl, or shell, spaced at regular intervals within the field tile.
- **Cut corner.** Usually a square field tile with two or more corners cut out to accommodate a key, or square insert, within.

But don't get distracted by exotic nomenclature. Focus your energy on deciding what overall style and vibe you are going for, and then envision ways of playing with shape and geometry to achieve it. You can even use standard field tile as an accent—you don't necessarily need a specialized piece.

One practical consideration: When mixing two or more types of tile within the same plane, make life much easier for your installer by sticking to tiles that are the same thickness as your field tile and that work within its modular dimensions. When accent pieces are thinner than the field tile, your installer must build up mortar behind to account for the height differential and create a level surface.

1. An animated confection of Pratt and Lambert ceramics dresses up a bath vignette. Although various tiles are used, the effect is harmonious thanks to careful adherence to a theme—nature—as well as a consistent richness to the glazes. **2.** A band of half-round liners creates the effect of a baseboard within a run of cast-ceramic tiles with medieval-style interlocking floral abstractions. **3.** Like a chair rail, a luminous band of multisized mosaics—the same used on the floor—divides a wainscot of gold-leaf-backed glass tiles from a swath of white ceramics. **4.** A border of multicolored 1-inch glass mosaics quietly emphasizes the fold where wall meets floor. Two sizes of slate on the walls and the floor inject additional variety.

1.

2.

3.

4.

Trim Pieces

Trims are used to punctuate a run of tile, accentuating or smoothing over the transition to another material—along wainscoting, where walls meet floor, along countertop edges, and so on. No matter which materials you are mixing or what overall style you are going for, a smooth flow from one material to another forms the basis of an artful and harmonious installation. The following trim pieces have specialized functions:

- A **bullnose** has one or more rounded edges to demarcate an expanse of tile with a smooth transition. It is most often used as a flourish to highlight the border between materials. Use a bullnose to end a run of tile wainscoting midway up a wall or to trace the edges of fireplaces.
- A **V-cap** is a V-shaped tile that wraps around the edge of a countertop, angling down toward the floor.
- **Base tiles** are the tile equivalent of wood baseboards. They run along the bottom of a wall, flush with a floor. **Crown moldings,** meanwhile, cap the top of a wall where it meets the ceiling.
- Akin to a bullnose, but symmetrical across its long axis, a **rail** culminates a run of tile, creating a sense of pause between two materials—or between two swaths of tile—not unlike a wooden chair rail.
- **Quarter-rounds** are curved elements placed where two perpendicular tiled surfaces meet.

You'll also have the option of less unusual-looking trims—flat tiles that are almost impossible to distinguish from regular field tile. Closer scrutiny, though, reveals that one or more edges of the trim tile are glazed. Use these like a bullnose along a wall—a more modern, less dramatic signoff—or to wrap corners, where the exposed rougher edge of a field tile would jar the overall composition.

When in doubt, have a showroom professional or an in-house designer help you navigate the seemingly endless combinations and permutations of trims and accents. Good salespeople are likely to point out any incompatibility in terms of materials and can demonstrate how to mix and match. They are also well versed in the intricacies of tile architecture and the elements necessary for a particular space.

Many manufacturers sell complete tile suites that include matching field tile, trims, and accents. Although you can certainly mix and match different makers' collections, this kind of one-stop shopping is a user-friendly option.

For more on trim pieces, see The Options, page 214 to 223.

Opposite: **In this classically detailed 1920s-inspired design, a rippled chair rail subtly articulates the dividing line. Although the design is quite polished and traditional, the absence of a base tile and the clean-lined chair rail keeps the décor from seeming overly fussy.**

1. 2.

A MODERN TWIST ON TRADITIONAL TRIMS

Dale Cohen may have learned a lot in architecture school, but Designing with Tile 101 was notably absent from her curriculum. "We were never taught anything about tile. You only learn on the job, and then only if you're really interested."

Something of a tile fanatic, she wanted the material to feature prominently in her own bathroom. But the room's diminutive dimensions posed a number of challenges. "New York City baths are so small," she explains. "I was insistent on having a stall shower *and* a tub because I wanted to feel like a grownup. But accommodating both is impossible unless you have a Rubik's Cube brain." Her tightly rejiggered floor plan showcased both of her desired features, but it left a number of visible nooks that were tricky to wrap tile around. "In a small space, every transition is visible, so pretty edges are vital." Here, she chose tiles glazed on one edge to create a refined look as they wrap around corners.

Her deft scheme makes the room feel large and luxe. The starting point was 3-centimeter mosaic flooring of hand-chopped Calacatta marble. "I initially sketched out a more interesting pattern," she says, "but I realized that the small room probably couldn't handle it. Typically you'd have 2-centimeter mosaics in a 1920s-influenced bathroom, but here I went up in scale because the room was so small. It's a misconception that small tiles enlarge a small room; large tiles have fewer busy grout lines, which cut up a space."

She paired the gray and white marble with ceramic tile in matching hues. The white planes are bordered with ribbed gray tiles: a single run atop the wainscoting, and stacked three-high at the bottom to mimic a traditional baseboard. "Trims can be blindingly expensive. And here, I preferred a more modern interpretation anyway, using old materials in a new way to create this quiet, feminine modernism." Old school and well schooled all in one.

3.

1. In Dale Cohen's 5½ by 10-foot bathroom, the walls are clad in horizontally stacked 4 by 16-inch white-body ceramic tiles. "Most ceramics have an orange or off-white bisque, which creates a yellow cast. For me, the bright-white body is one of those details that makes all the difference."
2. Cohen lucked out during the installation process. The room's dimensions worked with the 16-inch wall tile modules, requiring very few cut tiles—a benefit in a small space. "For installations needing a lot of cuts, I tend to order well over the standard 10 percent extra—sometimes as high as 20 percent. Here, though, that was unnecessary."
3. Gray grout highlights the sleek geometries. "I always use wide grout lines. Tile should look like tile, not a seamless ceramic wall." The gray ribbed trim tile was custom colored to match the marble veining.

The Aesthetics of Grout

Grout is, to many, a necessary evil: the adhesive that keeps tiles in place but inevitably gets dirty and dingy over time. For this reason, you may desire to downplay grout, and there are myriad ways to do so. Use larger tiles, which translates to fewer grout lines in a room. Depart from the standard ¼-inch lines and place the tiles closer together, making the crevices as skinny as structurally possible given your materials and finish. Choose a mellow, complementary color of grout that blends with the surrounding tile. Gravitate to cork or leather, which don't require grout at all. Or go for rectified tiles, which feature supersmooth edges so they can be installed in a butt-joined fashion (translation: with invisible grout lines).

The saying goes: The less grout, the less accumulation of dirt, which is mostly true. But today there are tough-as-nails epoxy-based grouts that are practically impermeable, and other stain-resistant formulations. The technology for grout has advanced significantly, meaning some of its perceived downsides are greatly diminished. In particular, no longer is the selection of grout colors limited to neutral grays and whites. Prettier decorative hues abound, thanks to special additives and pigments; you can even find speckly grouts that blend with the mottled look of terrazzo tile.

And beyond its utilitarian function, grout can be an inherently decorative tool if you know how to exploit it and are emboldened to do so. Subtler shades pull the color out of a tile, but grout that contrasts with the color of field tile imparts a more graphic look, highlighting the geometric rigor of the installation pattern. Or match grout exactly to the tile to form a continuous, monolithic surface; this is most easily achieved with textured tiles that mimic grout's cement-based character. Use an acid-bright grout against a neutral-colored tile for a little pop. Non-square shapes like octagons and circles can create the illusion of being set directly into a swath of grout. This way, the binder itself becomes the major design component.

Before you harness grout's expressiveness, it helps to learn a few basics concerning its composition, function, and structural capabilities. First of all—what is grout, exactly? It's a mixture of cement, sand, and water that fills the gap between tiles after they've been mortared to the underlying surface. Mortar holds the tiles down, but grout prevents them from moving laterally. Grout hardens and bonds with the

Opposite: **Narrow grout lines in a matching dark color allow this mural's watery black-and-gold swoosh to take center stage and read as a unified surface. When choosing grout width and color for tiles featuring continuous patterning, defer to a hue that blends with the field tile to ensure that the tiles remain the focal point.**

tile to hold it in place and protect the edges from moisture and damage; think of it as liquid concrete. Epoxy-based versions are available, too, although their fast bond makes them tougher to work with and consequently they are used less frequently in residential settings.

Grout gets protected with sealant, after which it should be well safeguarded from the buildup of soap scum, dirt, mildew, and mold. But over time, natural wear and tear

dulls grout's coloration and dirties its surface, and improper installation can lead to a number of undesirable conditions, from cracking to staining. The cement-based composition means it's susceptible to UV rays, so its color will bleed out eventually (or rapidly, if installed around an outdoor pool exposed to sunshine all year long). A perfect color match between tile and grout will fade; jet-black grout will pale to graphite gray over time. This is why many designers and installers advise clients to go darker than they might prefer. Very dark grout can stain some unglazed tiles, though, so be careful and test the combination before committing.

Once installed, grout can be replaced, although at some expense and with a certain degree of mess. You can also stain or paint grout, but the effect tends to diminish quickly and can look unprofessional. So make your initial choice carefully, because you should expect to live with your grout for a long time. Review colors against not only the tiles but also the rest of your décor: furnishings, fabrics, and paint colors, too.

Above: **To keep grout lines to a bare minimum, designer Jeff Miller clad the bathroom of his New York loft in oversized 24-inch squares of graphite-colored basalt. "Smaller tiles would have been more forgiving in a tight space, but this feels less 'bathroom-y,'" he says.**

The most resolved installations feature grout lines that are precisely even in width along each plane and that match up carefully where floors meet walls and walls meet ceilings. Sometimes floor and wall grout lines won't match up perfectly. To minimize this problem, consider alternating the installation pattern: Lay the same tiles diagonally on the wall and in a grid on the floor so you won't notice if the lines don't quite dovetail. Using a border piece to separate the swaths of tile where floors and walls meet also smooths things over.

Standard grout lines are ¼ inch wide, but you can often go fatter or thinner without compromising the integrity of the installation. For consistency, designers recommend keeping the grout thickness the same when mixing up the sizes and varieties of the tiles in a room. Also: For murals or tiles featuring a continuous decoration, grout should be as neutral as possible so as not to distract from the overall design.

Handpainted with a garden of florals, these ceramics from Bardelli make a colorful impression in a sunroom. The tiles are set close together, so the white grout doesn't distract from the composition.

Special Considerations

Locations where tile is subjected to extreme stresses—water, heat, sun, and gravity among them—demand top-performing materials and finishes.

Wet Areas: Showers and Pools

The primary considerations for wet areas—from showers and tub surrounds to steam rooms and pools—are slip resistance and imperviousness. Water resistance is not just a superficial issue but a deeper structural one as well. Certainly you don't want your tile staining from water, as many natural stones do even when sealed. But a waterproof space requires not just the right choice of surfacing material that will withstand liquid; it also necessitates a careful installation with the proper substrate and binders that work in concert as a moisture barrier to protect the underlying structure. Any water seeping behind the tile could affect the safety and integrity—and the beauty—of your design.

The two properties that qualify tile for a wet space don't always go hand in hand. Surfaces that repel liquid are often quite sleek, and thus slippery. Textured planes have more traction but are also more porous and generally harder to clean. Mother Nature hasn't yet reconciled this conundrum, but science has. Slip-resistant porcelains offer all the qualities you need: waterproof tile with an almost imperceptible texture that anchors feet yet is easily cleaned of soap scum and mildew. (Supporting systems such as ventilation and radiant heating can also go a long way toward alleviating moisture.)

When designing indoor and outdoor pools, account for any chemicals that may come into contact with the tiled surface—notably the chlorine or bromide that cleans the water, but also other harsh agents you may use to remove lime, calcium, or mildew. A pool is not the place for a porous material that absorbs moisture, nor is it an ideal environment for any natural stone, like marble, that reacts to such chemicals.

Outdoors, you must also factor in UV rays, which fade many tiles and grouts. Choose stable materials like ceramic and porcelain that won't be affected by sunlight. Other evils to contend with include dirt and sand.

There are two important terms to keep in mind for wet spaces:

- **Coefficient of friction.** Remember this from high-school science? It's a highfalutin term for the degree of traction a tile has underfoot. A high coefficient of friction means more friction, fewer slips.
- **Vitreous.** Ceramics and porcelains are also ranked according to imperviousness, from vitreous—the only category suited to a shower—to nonvitreous.

1. An indoor flume-style pool in the Wildwood, New Jersey, home of Bob and Ginny Blair is clad in a snappy porcelain that extends across the floor and up the surround. The wild, swirly pattern of the 12-inch tiles is tempered by the layout's rigorous grid. The owners tested a number of tiles before finding one with the right amount of grab underfoot. "I put water on samples in the showroom and walked on them in my bare feet," Ginny says. Radiant subfloor heating warms the room and hastens evaporation post-swim.

2. Architect René González designed a kidney-shaped pool for his Miami home. The pool's sinuous outline rises 1 foot above the surrounding lawn—a very dramatic move that also keeps grass cuttings and debris out of the water. González tiled the surround in colorful red and orange glass mosaics, which have withstood the harsh climate and beating sun. In his quest for a uniform look, he initially selected a red grout to match the tiles. Between the sun and the chlorine, though, the grout has faded to a less desirable but still lovely gray.

Fireplaces

A fireplace is an ideal canvas for tile experimentation. Spark up a plain-Jane design with a lively tile surround to convert a hole in the wall into an eye-catching architectural feature. Or highlight what is already the focal point of your living space by embellishing a mantel with tinted terra-cotta, adorning a surround with whimsical mosaics, or accentuating a vertical sweep of chimney with a graphic accent. You can even tile behind a freestanding stove, simultaneously accentuating its sculptural form and protecting surrounding surfaces from embers. There's logic behind the age-old tradition of tiled hearths. Aesthetics aside, the material protects timber-frame houses and drywall from soot and fire.

Perhaps your fireplace is already an assertive accent in its own right, complete with a mantel artfully clustered with *objets*. Then gravitate to a mellower design and rest assured that tile will provide a more protective buffer than drywall or wood. Better yet, clear off that mantel and use it to display the collection of tile samples you've been curating in anticipation of an upcoming renovation. Unmounted, loose tiles double as delightful artworks.

A fireplace has its own structural logic; it is divided into a series of surfaces: firebox, surround, hearth, mantel, and chimney. Cover each plane in a different tile variety for an active scheme or downplay clunky features and odd proportions by deploying a single material or color. Let the existing architecture guide you toward playing it up or toning it down, outlining or underscoring it.

Embrace the opportunity a fireplace provides to utilize tiles left over from other parts of the home. Or, on the other hand, view it as the perfect place to indulge in that expensive tile you weren't quite willing (or able) to spring for in larger amounts. Just make sure it's a durable variety.

There are functional and safety issues to consider when choosing tile for your fireplace. A wide hearth doesn't get much foot traffic, true, but it does get hot. Some tiles crack in high temperatures, while others, like leather and wood, expand or discolor. You may also be slinging—and dropping—heavy pieces of firewood onto the hearth or into the flames, to say nothing of dousing a fire with water on occasion.

Opposite: **Splurge on a coveted tile:** In her Malibu home, designer Nicole Sassaman tiled a curved wall above her walnut mantel in a mosaic of Jerusalem limestone. "The curve was originally drywall, which was so 1980s," she explains. "The tile makes the element look much more refined." Because she needed only a small amount of material to cover it, she embraced a luxe selection. "I love those limestone mosaics, but at sixty dollars a square foot, I needed to be judicious. If you have a tile you really love, find places like this to use it where it won't break the budget." And where you'll see—and enjoy—it often.

1. 2.

3.

Ceramic and porcelain are the strongest options; kiln-baked at high temperatures, they are impervious to flames. The firing process also leaves ceramic chemically inert so the material doesn't release toxic gas into the air, either. Terra-cotta and slate have proved tough in heat-intensive spaces. Many natural stones, however, darken and stain, so be sure to do your homework before buying.

Place sturdier tiles along lower elements like the surround and hearth and save the more fragile stuff for above the mantel, where heat and mechanical impact are lower. Fireboxes are best lined with unglazed ceramics that can take the heat, while on the exterior, a glazed surface is easier to clean soot from. To create a finished look, most designers recommend wrapping the exterior tile into the firebox or lining the edge in a bullnose tile; in this case, keep in mind that whatever you choose for the outside surface should be able to withstand the heat.

Installers typically use specialized heat-resistant mortars and substrates on fireplaces. You also must consult your local building department to ensure any alterations are up to code. Properly acclimate materials to the extreme conditions of heat before installation to avoid bubbling cork or cracking mosaics. Installers typically acclimate sensitive materials like leather to their surroundings prior to laying—but generally only to room temperature. When subjecting your tiles to the intense heat of a fireplace, you or your installer must expose them to those same conditions ahead of time.

Now that you've become knowledgeable about the intricacies and practicalities of putting together a design as well as the performance issues that will influence your search, you can learn the nuts and bolts of bringing your project to life—namely, how it gets installed. Then you'll be well equipped to start shopping the bountiful world of tile.

1. Turn a surround into an accent wall: Architect James Biber floated a concrete hearth against a shimmering wall of glazed bricks for the living area of a Montauk beach home. The feature wall becomes the accent rather than the fireplace, which Biber designed to quietly blend in; the tile and the raw concrete are similarly hued. 2. Use a single material to dramatic effect: One impactful idea is to clad the surround in a swath of one tile that imparts a strong character. Here, ¾-inch gold-leafed mosaics sparkle like flame—whether the fire is lit or not. Playing off the fireplace's superclean lines adds boldness without busyness. 3. Make creative use of leftovers: In the sitting room of their New Jersey beach house, Bob and Ginny Blair clad a gas-powered fireplace with tumbled limestone—extra tiles from their kitchen backsplash.

How It All Comes Together

This book presumes that you are using a professional installer, not tackling a tiled floor or patio as a DIY project. A few basics will help get you going and will demystify the process of shopping for, buying, and installing tile—all the invisible details that greatly affect the look of your design.

Shopping for Tile

Not so very long ago (twenty-five years, in fact), you couldn't even set foot in a tile showroom unless you were a professional installer or contractor. The consumer was banished behind the velvet rope. But the industry has changed enormously since then. The market has opened up to new materials, higher performance options, and a greater emphasis on decorative offerings, and has embraced a new audience: you. Showrooms now actively court end-users, exciting them about the possibility of the material. "The tile world was very hard-core until color tile came along and changed everything," explains Bob Niles, a master builder from Cape May, New Jersey. "Now the consumer is more involved in the selection process." Lucky you.

Although your installer generally still orders and pays for tile on your behalf, *you* get to do the shopping and specifying. You can walk into almost any showroom and peruse the vast quantity of items on display, whether you're on the hunt for inspiration or information. Many to-the-trade-only resources let you browse, too, although in most cases you'll need to work with an architect or designer if you decide to purchase the product.

The incredible variety of materials, styles, and formats can be daunting. Thankfully, salespeople are well versed in their wares and only too delighted to give you a tutorial, steering you in the right direction and helping refine your selection to something aesthetically and functionally appropriate. They can clarify whether a tile you're considering is tough enough to use on the floor or impervious enough for the

Opposite: The artistry for faux-bois porcelain tiles has advanced significantly, with more lifelike surface textures and grain patterns. Increasingly common are planklike shapes—such as these herringbone-patterned pavers from Kronos—which further disguise the material's high-tech character.

shower, and also help you pick the trims, insets, and bullnoses you'll need to compose your surfaces. Exploit their knowledge!

Some showrooms are more user-friendly than others. If yours sets out coffee and muffins in the morning and wine and cheese at sundown, you can probably rest assured you've found a place that encourages lingering and browsing. However, you don't need a lot of bells and whistles to have a good experience—just great products and helpful staff. If you find you're not getting good service or if you encounter a salesperson who's impatient with your questions, go elsewhere.

Lead Times

Beyond the basics of aesthetics and performance, you'll have to factor in the time that elapses between placing the order and its delivery. While many showrooms stock tiles in a nearby warehouse—meaning they can deliver within days if you wish—specialty items are often made or customized to your order. Any tile involving some degree of handcraftsmanship can easily take up to twelve or sixteen weeks. Hand-made items produced by small studios can vary quite drastically in color, size, and glaze. Because of this, you may be asked to approve a sample before the studio starts to fulfill the order. This step tacks on another few weeks.

Lead times can also be substantial for large-volume orders or stones that must be cut to size—sometimes three months or more for delivery. Depending on their location, some stone quarries shut during the winter months. If you place an order in November but your quarry is closed until spring, you are in for a long wait. For imported stones, which may come from as far away as Turkey, India, China, or Brazil, lead times are also contingent on how long it takes the boat to arrive at your shore and how frequently orders are batched and shipped in containers.

To avoid unwanted delays, work closely with your supplier. Ask about lead times *before* falling head over heels for a tile that can't ship for many moons—and that you need within a week. If time is of the essence, have a salesperson direct you to tiles carried in their stock program. It pays to plan ahead.

1. Gail Shields-Miller clad the walls of a guest bath with handmade ceramics textured to look like rice paper and inset with slim, hand-molded strips of the same material. 2. Andrea Di Giuseppe, the CEO of tile manufacturer Trend Group, used colorful glass mosaics to invigorate his Miami master bath. The dark color makes the main room seem cozy and cohesive, while the bright jolt of citrus hues makes the nooks feel more expansive. 3. Before committing to this particular color of honey onyx for the walls and floors of a New York bathroom, Peter Balsam reviewed samples in the client's home to find the one that worked best with the cabinetry. 4. With exotic natural stones like the 2-inch marble mosaics Shields-Miller used to floor her master bathroom, lead times must be taken into consideration.

1.

2.

3.

4.

Actual Versus Nominal Sizing

When buying tile, be attentive to sizing, as manufacturers follow one of two systems.

Some use standard sizing, which corresponds to the tile's exact dimensions; if you pull out a ruler, the measurement will match the listed size. Others companies, however, prefer nominal sizing, which is more of an approximation. Why? Generally to accommodate the additional width of grout lines (a 3⅞-inch-square tile to be installed with ¼-inch joints will have a nominal size of 4 inches) or to account for slight variations in size that occur during firing, particularly with hand-crafted tiles. While this matter is primarily your installer's concern, knowing about this before you walk into a showroom can help you avoid confusion later.

Sampling

By all means, get as many samples as you can and take them home with you. Smaller studios may charge a slight fee to send samples, but it's worth it. Much like paint, the color and tone of a tile—whether terra-cotta or lavastone or porcelain—may look quite different in your house than it does in the showroom. These traits vary with light conditions from morning to night and from season to season.

Scrutinize the color, texture, and finish where the tiles will eventually be installed. Prop them against walls or place them on the floor. Lean them against your countertop or your furnishings. This step is vital when purchasing brightly colored ceramics or vibrant stones—but also when choosing among subtle shades of beige and cream. To home in on the perfect hue, pick a few samples that are close in coloration and inspect them carefully in the context of your home.

The walls and floor of a shower are covered in a custom-cut stone mosaic from Artistic Tile that alternates 1-inch stripes of Azul Cielo, Bianco Antico, and Travertine Paglerino.

Variation

In addition to being judged for performance under certain high-stress conditions, most tiles are rated on a scale of 1 to 5 according to the degree of aesthetic variation expected within an order, 5 being the highest. Certain stones and artisanal products, like hand-molded, hand-glazed ceramics, tend to fall into the highest category, while neutral-hued machine-made porcelains are in the lowest. Your salesperson will likely address this concern as you focus your selection and might even show you physical examples of the degree of differentiation. But as you're shopping, bear in mind that the more "natural" a product is—even if man-made—the greater its variation from tile to tile and thus throughout a room.

Ordering

Responsibility for ordering building materials is best left to the person who's going to handle installation. In this case, you simply specify what you want and your contractor or subcontractor places the order, paying for the tile and including the price on your final bill.

Why should the installer order tile rather than you? Because the installer knows how to measure your floor or wall or room to ensure that the proper amount of material is ordered for your particular location, factoring in issues like out-of-plumb walls and tricky conditions requiring numerous cuts. He also inspects the tiles and arranges for their delivery to your house. If anything goes wrong with the order—from damage to an off-color batch to the wrong tiles entirely—he can address the problem. Tiles damaged during shipment can be replaced, of course, but receiving new ones can take days or weeks, and materials should be reordered well in advance of installation. (You never want to discover a box of broken tiles midway through the tiling process; the cost of stopping and restarting the job is prohibitive.)

Tile also weighs a ton and is often shipped in large boxes or crates that prove unwieldy for your average home owner to grapple with. Shopping for tile is not like shopping for dining room chairs. A building product that becomes a structural part of your house, tile falls into the same category as lumber and drywall—materials you would probably never consider buying yourself.

Installers measure based on the surface area—taking all the nooks and crannies into account—and throw in a little extra for good measure. The guideline is to order 10 percent more than the actual square footage, an amount that accounts for damaged tiles or ones that are slightly off-color. If the materials have a high degree of natural variation, like stone, or if the installation is particularly tricky or involves a number of cut tiles—as with diagonal patterns or large-format tiles—experts advise ordering even more, sometimes up to 20 percent over the actual square footage.

You want all your stone to come from the same lot; this ensures that one side of your floor won't be much lighter and more patterned than the other. Placing orders even a week apart can make a difference. Indeed, matching tiles to earlier batches, dye lots, or stone lots can be difficult. Within reason, buy as much overage as you can, all at once, so you will have matching extras if you need to replace any tiles once they are installed. While some showrooms let you return—and give you a refund for—extra tiles, this is the exception, and few will let you return natural stone. But a little extra tile can be a good thing; many designers encourage their clients to buy as much overage as they can afford (or have room to store), particularly with handmade tiles and batch-dyed leather. To guarantee a perfect match in the event of future damage, maintain a small stockpile.

Pricing

A little word on pricing: Tiles are generally priced per square foot, although artisans sometimes charge per tile. Prices can start as low as $1.99 and the upper limit is, well, essentially limitless. A $110-per-square-foot handmade glass backsplash is not unheard of, and patterned mosaics can be quite pricey too. High-performance porcelain is more expensive than ceramic. And certain stones can be exorbitant, particularly if they are exceedingly rare or no longer quarried.

But there are many beautiful options in a relatively affordable $5 to $10 range. While there are ways to save money, skimping on your installer is not one of them. Here are a few alternatives:

1. **LOOK FOR REMNANTS.** Small batches of tile left over from larger jobs are often quite affordable, especially if you need only a few square feet for a backsplash.

2. **USE PRICEY TILE IN SMALL AMOUNTS.** But use it where it's most visible—fireplace surrounds, staircase risers, ledges, accent walls, or inset into a field of an inexpensive tile.

3. **CHOOSE FAUX OVER REAL.** Stonelike porcelains and agglomerates are often less expensive than their natural counterparts—and more durable, too.

4. **HAVE TILE CUT DOWN TO SIZE BY YOUR INSTALLER.** Generally, the smaller the tile, the more expensive; the same material in a 12-inch square is less expensive than it is in a 4-inch size. You can order large and have your installer cut the pieces down. But proceed with caution: Do this only if you don't mind that the edges of your tiles won't be as crisply finished, with glazing that curls over the edge; there is a reason cut tiles are placed along the periphery of a floor or wall, where the rougher side can be hidden below a baseboard or under furniture.

5. **KEEP THE BIG PICTURE IN MIND.** Tile may cost more up front, but it can save you money in the long run. A durable tiled surface, if installed properly and suited to its application, can stand up well over many years and require much less maintenance than other materials. And if you choose right, you'll have a timeless, enduring look.

Installation

The experts agree: A superior installation is the secret to a successful design, one that's both durable and aesthetically appealing. A solid substrate, deftly applied setting materials, and placement of tiles to maximize composition and minimize cut lines—such details make all the difference on your floors and walls.

When thinking about your tiled surface, recall the whimsical tale of the princess and the pea. One small flaw below—a wobbly joist, a sloppily applied thinset—can be telegraphed through layers of mortar and waterproofing membranes and greatly affect the surface. If the underlying substrate expands or contracts, the tiles can crack and flat planes can buckle. Water can even seep through to compromise the beauty and integrity of your patio or shower floor. A chain is as strong as its weakest link; likewise, a tiled plane is only as solid as what lies beneath.

As for surface matters like aesthetics, a good installation is distinguished by grout lines of a consistent width, grout color chosen to complement tiles, unobtrusive placement of cut tiles, graceful treatment along corners and where two surfaces meet, and properly centered floor tiles. Heavily patterned natural stones like Carrara marble should have a poetic flow of veins, swooshes, and speckles. Trim tiles should smoothly finish corners and wall edges. Such minutiae separate an excellent installation—and installer—from a subpar one.

The Home Owner's Role

Where does the home owner factor into this equation? Once equipped with the basics, should you hover over your installer and comment on how he's placing the cut tiles? This is not advisable unless you, too, are a professional of the trade. However, your contractor is generally on site to oversee the tile installation, and designers and architects often supervise tricky installations to advise on aesthetic matters.

Be sure you, your designer, and your installer are on the same page in terms of how the room should look, especially when using irregular tiles in unique applications. Everything from grout joints to pattern layouts should be discussed beforehand. If a backsplash or a floor is going to receive particuarly hard wear, let your installer know. If you want to avoid cut tiles along a certain prominent wall—perhaps where people enter a room—speak up.

Opposite: In a Los Angeles guest bath, designer Jeff Andrews tiled the walls, floor, and open shower in 1-inch mosaics, intermingling shimmery tiger's-eye, brown, and pale blue glass. (Prolific grout lines make the shiny surfaces less slippery underfoot.) The continuous expanses of translucent tile convert the room into a seamless wet space and magnify the intensity of natural light.

Two things you, the tile owner, are in charge of:

- Stay off floors for twenty-four to seventy-two hours **postinstallation.** Furniture should not be placed until the tiles have had a chance to set. Avoid spilling wine on a tiled countertop or backsplash with unsealed grout.
- **Maintenance.** All tiles require periodic maintenance, from cleaning to occasional resealing to refinishing.

Words from the Wise

Common mistakes, cautionary tales, and helpful hints for achieving a beautiful installation:

1. **CHECK SAMPLES (OF TILE AND GROUT) IN CONTEXT.** Tile is like wall paint or upholstery fabric—colors, textures, and finishes can look surprisingly different once you take them home with you. What appears creamy beige in the showroom can take on a yellow cast in your living room. A sprightly forest green tile chosen for your backsplash veers toward blue when placed beside your marble countertop. A honed finish seems more polished in different lighting. To avoid any such surprises, review samples exactly where they'll be installed for the most accurate approximation of what the tile will look like once it is permanently affixed to your wall or floor. If grout is a major component of your design, review grouted tile samples on site, too.

Colors and finishes change appearance according to natural and artificial illumination. Do you tend to use overhead track lights or floor and table lamps? Incandescent or halogen? Check your tiles under these conditions. Bear in mind that the character, intensity, and angle of sunlight also changes daily and seasonally. If you are selecting tiles for the floor of your summer beach house, review samples in the home during summer months for the truest reflection of the results. Of course, this only works if you plan way in advance. But if you're initiating a major renovation or new construction, it's worth considering this level of detail.

2. **SAVE ON MATERIALS; SPLURGE ON INSTALLATION.** Don't skimp where it matters—on the person responsible for laying out your tile. Find a talented and responsible soul who won't rush the job and won't cut corners. Avoid anyone who tells you that tile can be installed in a day; it can't.

Variegated natural stones that are not of uniform thickness are excruciating to install. Some slate tiles, for instance, come in odd thicknesses and dimensions, often varying from one edge to the other by more than ¼ inch. These need to be dry-laid in advance and the mortar bed properly built up to account for the height differential. This meticulous process can slow progress to just a handful of tiles installed per day. It is not a job to take lightly, and an exemplary tile contractor never rushes.

Irregularly shaped handmade tiles can prove tricky, too, especially when you wish to avoid cutting them along the edges of a room. In this case, the wall can be floated—that is, a new wall built over the existing one and designed to the exact dimensions of the tile, rather than the reverse. Such invisible but exacting detail takes longer—at least a few days, and you'll lose a few inches of square footage—but pays off with a harmonious composition.

3. COORDINATE INSTALLATION THROUGH YOUR CONTRACTOR. If you are planning a small job—tiling a backsplash, redoing the floor of a petite powder room—you may be tempted to have your showroom coordinate the installation. While suppliers do have talented tradespeople in their stable (and, indeed, many high-end specialty showrooms recommend using their installer), this is not the preferred course of action. Even small-scale jobs can require structural work that extends beyond the scope of a tile installer. And, more to the point, the economics of hiring an installer through your showroom do not fall in your favor; the showroom is likely to outsource the job to the cheapest bid to make the most money. Your own contractor, designer, or builder is a much safer bet for completing the job to your high standards and negotiating in the event of surprises like discovering a compromised subfloor that must be relaid, adding extra time and expense. Such structural issues fall in the hands of your contractor, whose responsibility it is to build a sound canvas for the tile.

Quick Fixes

If you're not up for the hassle of replacing existing stone or tile (it is a messy and labor-intensive process, after all) some tasteful alternatives prove relatively painless while still providing opportunities for creative experimentation. Best of all, by reusing what's already in place rather than tearing it out, these options divert waste from the landfill.

Regrouting

Whether your grout is stained or discolored or you've simply fallen out of love with the slightly bold hue you chose some years ago, regrouting may offer the perfect solution, particularly if the tiles themselves are in sound shape and could just use a little enhancement.

Leave regrouting to professionals; there are companies who specialize in the service. The process entails scooping out much of the old grout with a small abrasive blade, cleaning the tiled surface, applying the new material, and then sealing it. Regrouting can be messy—it tends to stir up a fair amount of dust—and laborious. But it's doable in just a matter of days, and the results can be enduring and remarkably transformative.

A few caveats: Epoxy-based grouts are much harder—and thus harder to remove—than standard cement-based ones. Also, unglazed tiles and natural stones like tumbled marble tend to absorb more grout to begin with, so the grout is best attacked with a saw. Otherwise, you risk chipping the tile.

Refinishing Stone

Hate the shiny black granite–tiled backsplash your home's previous owner installed? Take heart: It may not be a lost cause. Some particularly assertive limestones and dated granites can, if honed down, look like another material entirely. Remember, a stone's appearance differs significantly depending on the finish, particularly with the most animated varieties. Highly polished granite refinished to a matte, honed texture can be mistaken for a mellow black limestone.

Refinishing is not always cheap or easy. Know beforehand what you are getting into: Have the refinisher execute a spot test before tackling the entire surface. Otherwise, you might find yourself as disappointed with the results as with the original.

Porcelain Coating

Do those pink bathroom tiles make you feel as though you are living in a 1970s time warp? If you're not up to the task of tearing them out, you can porcelain-coat the existing tiled surface—the same process you'd use to make over a dingy clawfoot tub or a stained sink. It's possible to porcelain-coat your shower or even tiled kitchen countertops.

This relatively easy process involves spraying the tiled surface, grout and all, with a nonporous enamel-based paint. It even covers cracks. This is not a DIY project, however. Tiles should be properly cleaned of soap scum, mold, and mildew and then assessed for underlying structural issues. It's easy to find local professionals, and the service is relatively cheap and quick (especially compared to installing new tile).

Porcelain coats come in a wide range of colors and are also customizable. But designers often recommend sticking with white or another neutral to achieve the most natural results, since you'll be porcelain-coating the grout, too.

Left: Glass tiles like the snow-white mosaics covering the walls and floor of this Montauk bath often require special silicone binders.

After digesting these vital nuts and bolts about how an installation comes together, how to work with a showroom, and some of the structural and procedural issues you may face, it's time to start looking at product and choosing which tiles will work best for your particular application and aesthetic. Looking, after all, makes the project a less abstract proposition. And it's the best way to figure out what you really want—you may be surprised at what piques your interest and curiosity.

the options

The most effective (and entertaining) way to find a tile variety that's best suited to your needs, your taste, and your heart's desire is to dive right in. Immerse yourself in the more than a thousand examples we've assembled—from citrus-hued hand-poured glass to light-conducting acrylic polymer—organized by shape, material, color, character, function, and more. Let the ones that speak to you inspire and guide your further investigation. Enjoy!

Manufacturers Key

The initials in red next to each caption indicate the manufacturer or supplier of the tile shown. For more information, see Resources starting on page 303.

ABK=ABK Group Industrie Ceramiche
AD=Antiqua Domus
AS=Ann Sacks
AT=Artistic Tile
ATL=Ceramiche Atlas Concorde
BAR=Ceramica Bardelli
BI=Bisazza
CAM=Ceramica Campani
CC=Cerim Ceramiche
CDC=Casa Dolce Casa
CEVI=CE.VI Ceramica Vietrese
COE=Ceramiche Coem
COT=Cotto Veneto
CS=Costello Studio
CV=Ceramica Viva
DB=Dan Bleier
DE=Dirk Elliot Tile Co.
DEB=Decoratori Bassanesi
DIA= Cerámicas Diago
DU=Dune
DUC=Duca di Camastra
ECT=Eliane Ceramic Tiles

ED=Etruria Design
EG=Edilgres-Sirio Ceramiche
EI=Eleek Inc.
EL=Edelman Leather
FIO=Ceramica Fioranese
FG=Floor Gres
GA=Gayafores
GT=Granada Tiles
HTB=Hastings Tile & Bath
IZ=Iznik Tiles and Ceramic Corporation
JMS=Jason Miller Studio
KR=Kronos Ceramiche
LC=Lea Ceramiche
LMM=La Moderna Manifattura
MA=Majorca
MAM=Made a Mano
MAR=Bi Marmi
MAT=Matter
MC=Marca Corona
MIO=MIO
MOD=ModCraft
MR=Maya Romanoff

MT=Motawi Tileworks
NO=Novoceram
NT=Native Trails
NTC=Nemo Tile Company
OG=Oceanside Glasstile
PC=Petracer's Ceramics
PD=Popham Design
PER=Peronda
PRO=Ceramiche Provenza
RA=Ragno
RCA=Rex Ceramiche Artistiche
SEN=SensiTile Systems
SET=Ceramiche Settecento Valtresinaro
SI=Sicis
SLN=Studio Le Nid
SS=Stone Source
TIC=Ticsa America
TAN=Tanimar
TR=Trend
TRE=Ceramica di Treviso
TT=Trikeenan Tileworks
TU=Tulikivi
UA=Urban Archaeology
VAL=Valpanaro Candia
VI=Vidrotil
WZ=Walker Zanger
XT=Xenia Taler Design

MATERIALS

Marvel at the breadth of materials at your disposal—from cement and concrete to cork and other eco-friendly options—as well as the surprising variety of styles even within these categories. Discover how metal can look shiny and sleek or luxuriously soft depending on the composition and finish, as well as how ceramics range from earthy, rustic terra-cotta to geometrically mod shapes with contemporary flair. For information on the advantages, installation considerations, and care of many of the materials shown, see chapter 2, "Narrowing In," page 57.

cement and concrete

20-cm-sq handmade Moroccan cement PD

20-cm-sq handmade
Moroccan cement PD

20-cm-sq handmade
Moroccan cement PD

20-cm-sq handmade
Moroccan cement PD

30-cm-sq cement
agglomerate CDC

12 x 14-in concrete AS

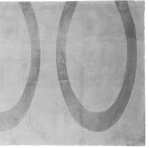

20-cm-sq handmade
Morrocan cement PD

20-c m-sq handmade
Moroccan cement PD

20-cm-sq handmade
Moroccan cement PD

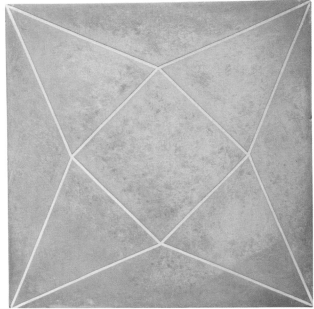

12-in-sq concrete AS

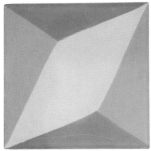

6-in-sq handmade cement
UA

4-in-sq cement GT

8-in-sq handmade cement
UA

6-in-sq handmade cement
UA

12-in-sq concrete AS

12-in-sq concrete AS

12-in-sq concrete AS

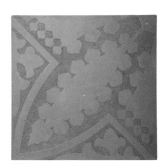

12-in-sq concrete AS

stone

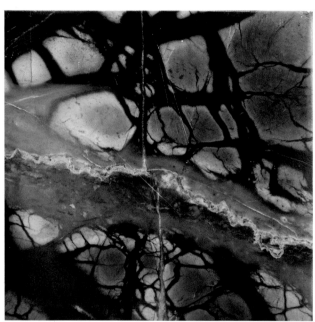

2-in-sq Picasso marble UA

2 × 4-in onyx mosaic NTC

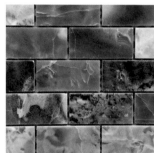

2 × 4-in blue onyx mosaic NTC

3 × 6-in to 1 × 6-in Crema Marfil mosaic NTC

2 × 4-in onyx mosaic NTC

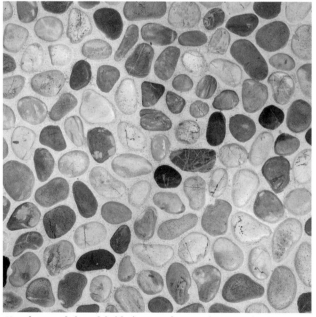

Hand-sorted, hand-laid river-rock mosaic on 12-in-sq mesh-backed sheets NTC

12-in-sq onyx AT

12-in-sq polished silver onyx AT

12 × 24-in Ocean Blue travertine AT

12-in-sq natural-cleft Ivory Dove slate AT

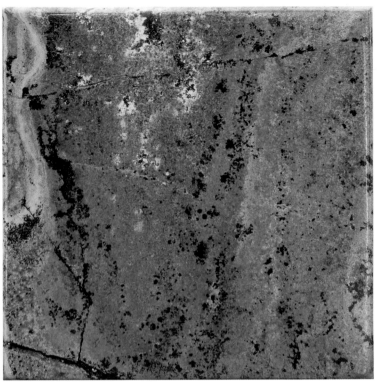

2-in-sq malachite UA

1-in-sq soapstone mosaic TU

¾-in-sq onyx mosaic NTC

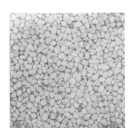

12-in-sq Bianco Carrera marble in resin AT

12-in-sq river stones in resin AT

2-in-sq etched limestone mosaic NTC

48-in-sq marble mosaic medallion UA

8 × 12-in etched, stained dark travertine UA

4-in-sq etched, stained chocolate travertine UA

6-in-sq etched, stained dark travertine tiles UA

4 × 12-in etched, stained Jerusalem limestone liner UA

7-in-sq engraved, filled
travertine AT

4-in-sq etched Jerusalem
stone UA

2½-in-sq etched, stained
travertine UA

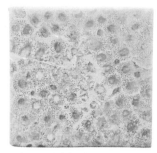

2-in-sq Philippine brown
fossil coral UA

12-in-sq Aquatina-etched limestone TR

8 × 12-in etched Jerusalem limestone UA

4-in-sq acid-etched, metal-
leafed natural-cleft Brazilian
slate AT

3-in-sq etched, stained
travertine UA

8 × 12-in etched, hand-painted antiqued Jerusalem
limestone UA

Breccia Fawahkir quartzite (12-in-sq detail) SS

16 × 24-in limestone TR

2-in-sq and 2 × 6-in white-gold quartz mosaic SS

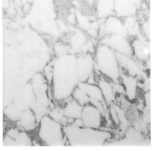

16-in-sq Cerviole marble SS

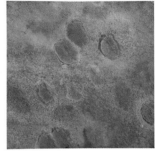

12-in-sq Westcountry slate SS

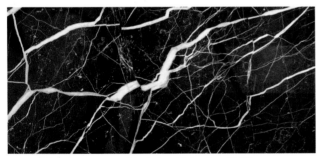

New Saint Laurent marble (12 × 20-in detail) SS

Cippolino marble (12-in-sq detail) SS

Orian Blue marble (12-in-sq detail) SS

16-in-sq Tiger Skin travertine SS

6 × 24-in Stalatitti Gold marble SS

6 × 24-in Stalatitti Gold marble SS

12 × 24-in Giallo Etrusco marble SS

12 × 24-in Muyu Brown marble SS

6 × 24-in brushed, unfilled Tango travertine AT

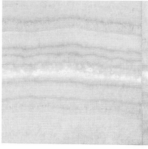

12-in-sq Honey onyx AT

16-in-sq Blu Masaccio marble SS

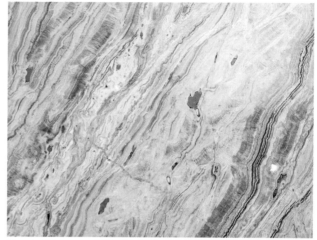

Esmeralda onyx (12 × 20-in detail) SS

⅝-in-sq and ⅝ × 12-in acid-etched, gold-leafed Thassos marble AT

12-in-sq hand-cut, hand-painted, Aquatina-etched limestone TR

12-in-sq Stellar white marble SS

stone continued

15 × 24-in antiqued Jerusalem limestone AT

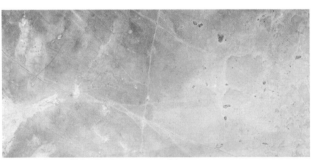

12 × 24-in polished Thassos marble AT

12-in-sq Bianco onyx AT

6-in-sq Bianco Antico marble AT

2-in-sq Honey onyx pillow mosaic on 6-in-sq netted sheets AS

12-in-sq Indian slate AS

1 × 3-in statuary white marble mosaic NTC

12 × 24-in Azul Macuaba marble AT

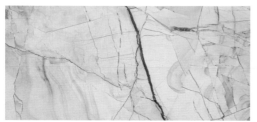

Burma Teak marble (12 × 20-in detail) SS

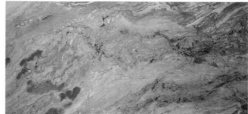

Mayan Sunset (12 × 20-in detail) SS

12-in-sq soapstone TU

12 × 24-in Linac marble SS

12 × 24-in Teakwood marble AT

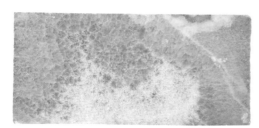

3 × 6-in Sable onyx AT

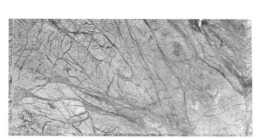

12 × 24-in Rainforest Brown marble AT

Persian Red travertine (12 × 20-in detail) SS

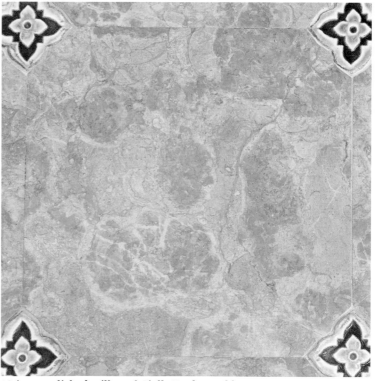

12-in-sq polished, pillowed Giallo Reale marble AT

leather

18-in-sq leather EL

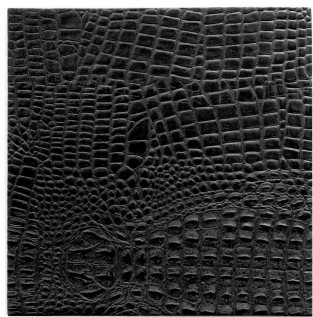

14-in-sq embossed leather AS

8-in-sq crocodile-embossed
leather UA

4-in-sq boar-print leather EL

4-in-sq boar-print leather
EL

4-in-sq antiqued leather
EL

8-in-sq embossed leather
UA

14-in-sq hand-dyed, hand-stamped Herman Oak leather AS

14-in-sq hand-dyed, hand-stamped Herman Oak leather AS

9¾-in-sq embossed leather CS

2 × 8-in parquet-pattern leather EL

9¾-in-sq embossed leather CS

9¾-in-sq embossed leather CS

4-in-sq leather EL

4-in-sq leather EL

9¾-in-sq embossed leather CS

9¾-in-sq embossed leather CS

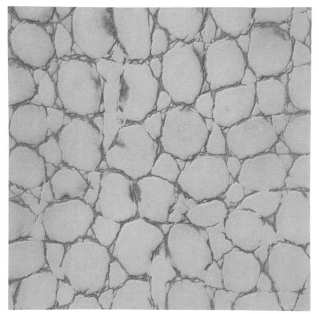

4-in-sq antiqued leather EL

12-in-sq leather EL

4-in-sq leather EL

4-in-sq leather EL

14-in-sq hand-dyed, hand-stamped Herman Oak leather AS

4-in-sq leather AS

1½ × 12-in leather trim AS

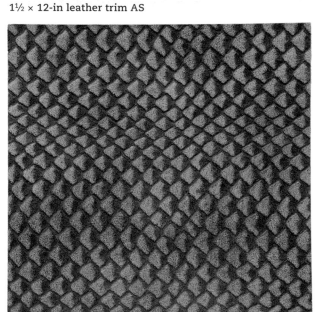

4-in-sq snake-print leather EL

4-in-sq boar-print leather EL

4-in-sq leather EL

4-in-sq snake-print leather EL

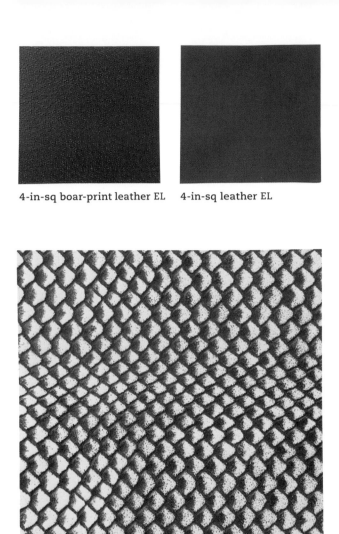

4-in-sq snake-print leather EL

4-in-sq leather EL

4-in-sq leather EL

4-in-sq boar-print leather EL

wood

4-in-sq pillowed mesquite AS

¾ × 2¾-in cross-cut honey pine mosaic AT

2 × 8-in mesquite tiles in varying thicknesses AS

3 × 5¾-in mesquite AS

1-in-sq and 1 × 2-in rosewood and teak mosaic UA

4-in-sq mesquite tiles in varying thicknesses AS

2 × 8-in mesquite AS

4-in-sq mesquite AS

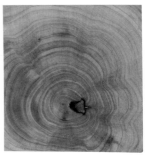

2-in-sq cross-cut honey pine mosaic AT

metal

1⅛-in-diameter bronze AS

6-in-sq handcrafted
cast metal AT

4-in-sq handcrafted
cast metal AT

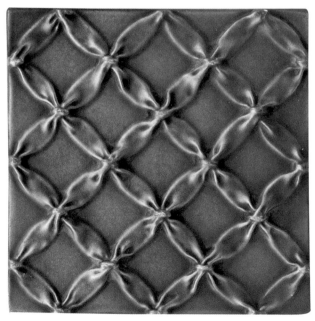

2½-in-sq cast bronze AT

1¾-in-sq handcrafted cast
metal AT

6-in-sq handcrafted cast metal AT

3-in-sq bronze AS

2-in-sq bronze AS

2-in-sq bronze AS

2-in-sq bronze AS

2¾-in-diameter bronze AS

¾ × 8-in handcrafted cast metal trims AT

1-in-sq handcrafted cast metal AT

¾ × 1⅛-in gold-finished
stainless-steel mosaic SS

1³⁄₁₆-in-sq brass-finished
stainless-steel mosaic SS

30-cm-sq metal LMM

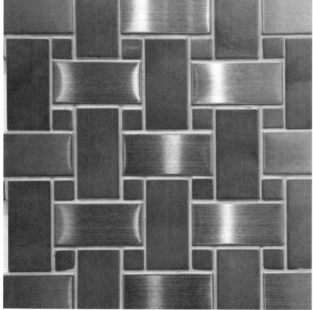

Multisized copper-finished stainless-steel mosaic SS

¾-in-diameter brushed stainless-steel penny rounds AS

⅜ × 1⅛-in gold-finished
stainless-steel mosaic SS

2 × 2-in and 2 × 6-in copper mosaic AS

¾-in-diameter copper-
finished stainless-steel
penny rounds SS

1¼-by ¾-in gold-finished stainless-steel mosaic SS

⅜ × 1⅛-in nickel-finish stainless-steel mosaic SS

3-in-sq and 1½ × 3-in stainless steel UA

⅜ × 1⅛-in gold-finished stainless-steel mosaic SS

2-in-sq cast bronze decos and liners AS

3-in-sq and 1½ × 4-in bronze UA

2 × 6-in bronze AT

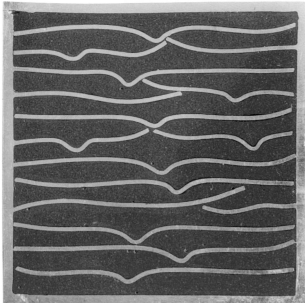

2-in-sq enamel-on-metal cloisonné AS

12-in-sq hand-inlaid paper-backed metal MR

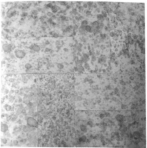

12-in-sq hand-inlaid paper-backed metal MR

12-in-sq hand-inlaid paper-backed metal MR

12-in-sq hand-inlaid paper-backed metal MR

1 × 6-in enamel-on-metal cloisonné AS

12-in-sq hand-inlaid paper-backed metal MR

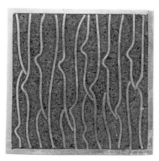

2-in-sq enamel-on-metal cloisonné AS

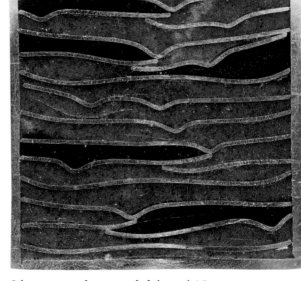

2-in-sq enamel-on-metal cloisonné AS

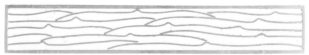

1 × 6-in enamel-on-metal cloisonné AS

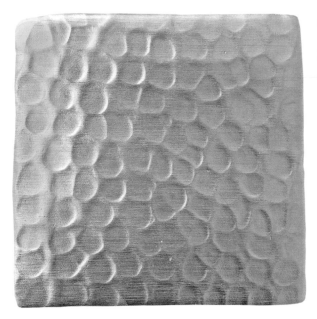

4-in-sq brushed-nickel finish copper NT

2¼ × 5¾-in bronze trim AS

6-in-sq bronze AT

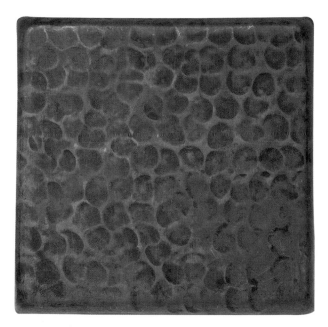

4-in-sq antique-finished copper NT

Custom-sized pewter molding (2 × 4-in detail) UA

metal continued

2½-in-sq white bronze UA

2 × 6-in bronze AT

2-in-sq bronze AT

2-in-sq cast bronze AS

2-in-sq handcrafted
cast metal AT

2 × 6-in enameled bronze
AT

6-in-sq handcrafted metal
AT

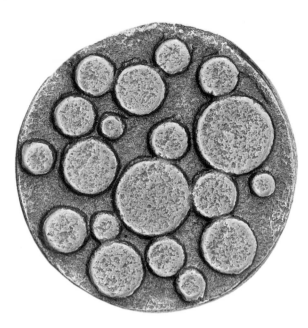

1½-in-diameter cast bronze
AS

4-in-sq recycled aluminum
EI

2½ × 6-in bronze liner AS

4-in-sq recycled aluminum
EI

2½-in-sq enameled bronze AT

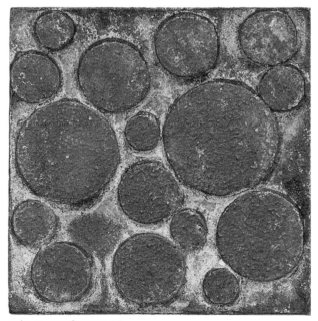

1-in-sq cast bronze AS

glass

¼ × 2-in mini-brick glass mosaic NTC

Custom-sized handmade
glass mosaic DB

Custom-sized back-leafed
glass mosaic DB

Custom-sized handmade
glass mosaic DB

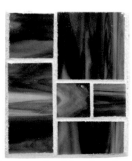

Custom-sized handmade
glass mosaic DB

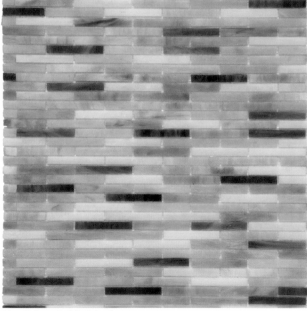

¼ × 2-in mini-brick glass
mosaic NTC

1 × 2-in glass mosaic NTC

Custom-sized handmade glass mosaic DB

1-in-diameter glass penny rounds NTC

2 × 8-in glass NTC

4-in-sq glass TR

1½ × 3-in glass mosaic TR

⅝-in-sq glass mosaic SI

3 × 12-in glass liner HTB

3 × 12-in glass liner HTB

Multisized beach glass mosaic UA

2 × 4-in textured matte glass NTC

1-in-sq recycled-glass mosaic SS

1-in-sq hand-cast, hand-cut recycled molten glass mosaic OG

1-in-sq hand-cast, hand-cut recycled molten glass mosaic OG

¾-in-sq ladle-poured, hand-cut glass mosaic VI

¾-in-sq ladle-poured, hand-cut glass mosaic VI

Custom-sized handmade back-leafed glass mosaic DB

¾-in-sq ladle-poured, hand-cut glass mosaic VI

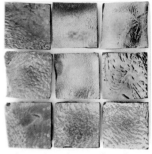

1-in-sq hand-cast, hand-cut recycled molten glass mosaic OG

¾-in-sq glass mosaic BI

4-in-sq glass AT

4-in-sq glass AT

¾-in-sq glass mosaic BI

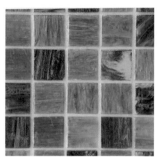

¾-in-sq glass mosaic BI

1-in-sq glass mosaic OG

Custom-sized back-leafed
glass mosaic DB

12-in-sq leaf-backed shattered glass AT

2 × 8-in shattered glass AT

3 × 9½-in glass TR

½-in-sq Venetian enamel glass mosaic (detail)

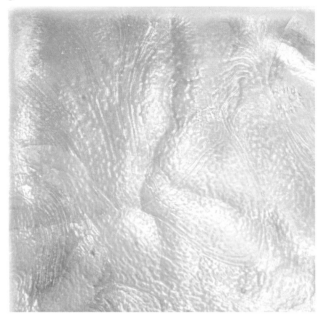

10-in-sq hand-cast, hand-cut recycled molten glass OG

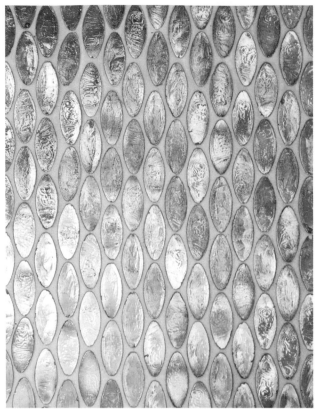

Multisized glass mosaic on 12-in sheets SI

Custom-sized etched glass AT

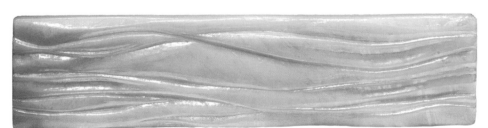

9½ × 2½-in hand-cast, hand-cut recycled molten glass trim OG

5 × 10-in hand-cast, hand-cut recycled molten glass OG

2 × 4-in glass AT

2 × 4-in glass AT

Handcrafted, hand-colored glass pebble mosaic on 4-in-sq sheets NTC

¾-in-sq glass mosaic BI

¾-in-sq glass mosaic BI

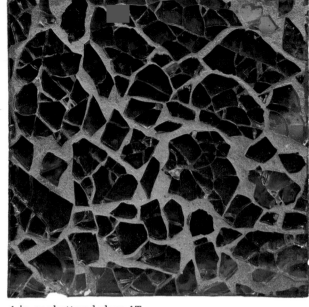

4-in-sq shattered glass AT

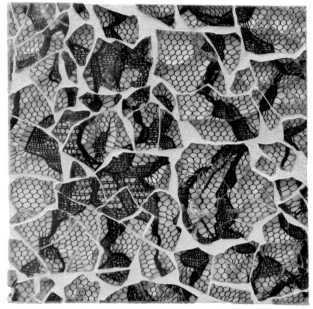

4-in-sq lace-backed
shattered glass AT

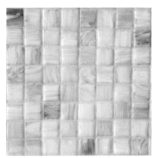

⅜-in-sq glass mosaic BI

¾-in-sq glass mosaic BI

4-in-sq lace-backed
shattered glass AT

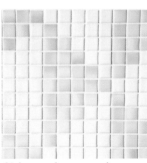

¾-in-sq glass mosaic
(detail) BI

¾-in-sq glass mosaic BI

9½-in-sq glass SS

4-in-sq metal-leaf-backed glass AT

4-in-sq metal-leaf-backed glass AT

4-in-sq metal-leaf-backed glass AT

4-in-sq metal-leaf-backed glass AT

12-in-sq shattered glass AT

5-in-sq hand-cast, hand-cut recycled molten iridescent glass OG

4½ × 13½-in European gold–leafed handcrafted glass AS

6-in-sq European gold–leafed handcrafted glass AS

9½-in-sq glass SS

9½-in-sq glass SS

2-in handmade quilted-glass mosaic on 12-in-sq sheets AS

¾ × 1½-in handmade quilted-glass mosaic on 12-in-sq sheets AS

10-in-sq hand-cast, hand-cut recycled molten iridescent glass OG

3-in-sq handmade recycled-content glass relief tile with hand-broken edge AS

ceramic continued

4⅛-in-sq handmade ceramic NTC

8-in-sq ceramic HTB

8-in-sq ceramic HTB

4⅛-in-sq handmade ceramic NTC

4⅛-in-sq handmade
ceramic NTC

4⅛-in-sq handmade
ceramic NTC

4⅛-in-sq handmade
ceramic NTC

8-in-sq ceramic HTB

½-in-sq high-fired ceramic
mosaic NTC

15-cm glazed *terra cotto*
MAM

5-in-sq ceramic HTB

20-cm-sq handmade, hand-painted ceramic DUC

3 × 6-in hand-molded,
tumbled-edge ceramic
subway tile NTC

3 × 6-in hand-molded,
tumbled-edge ceramic
subway tile NTC

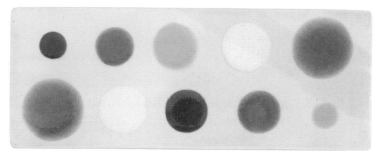

4 × 10-in hand-painted glazed ceramic XT

8-in-sq ceramic HTB

6-in-sq extruded
ceramic CDC

6-in-sq extruded
ceramic CDC

6-in-sq extruded
ceramic CDC

4 × 8-in ceramic UA

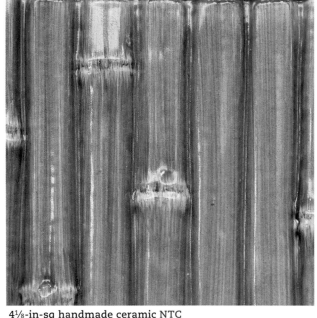

4⅛-in-sq handmade ceramic NTC

4-in-sq handcrafted glazed ceramic AT

4-in-sq handcrafted glazed ceramic AT

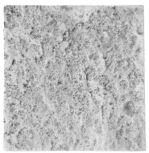

4-in-sq handcrafted glazed ceramic AT

4-in-sq handcrafted glazed ceramic AT

1 × 6-in, 2-in-sq, and 3-in-sq handcrafted, wood-fired glazed ceramics UA

4-in-sq handcrafted ceramic AT

4-in-sq handcrafted glazed ceramic AT

8-in-sq ceramic HTB

8-in-sq ceramic HTB

8-in-sq ceramic HTB

8-in-sq ceramic HTB

4-in-sq glazed ceramic UA

6-in-sq handmade ceramic
UA

6-in-sq handmade ceramic
UA

8-in-sq ceramic (detail) HTB

4-in-sq handcrafted glazed
ceramic AT

30-cm-sq handmade, hand-painted ceramic DUC

36-in-sq lavastone panel AD

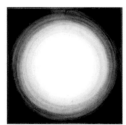

20-cm-sq handmade ceramic AD

5 × 10-in ceramic HTB

20-cm-sq glazed ceramic DEB

15-cm-sq handcrafted *cotto* tiles SLN

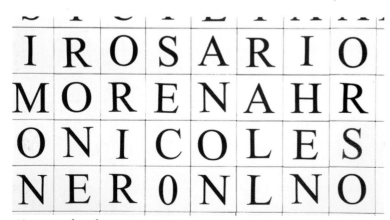

10-cm-sq glazed *terra cotto* MAM

3 × 6-in handmade, hand-painted ceramic DUC

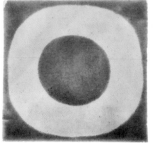

4-in-sq hand-painted glazed ceramic XT

4-in-sq hand-painted glazed ceramic XT

4-in-sq hand-painted glazed ceramic XT

15-cm-sq handcrafted *cotto* tiles SLN

4-in-sq hand-painted glazed ceramic XT

4-in-sq hand-painted glazed ceramic XT

4-in-sq glazed ceramic UA

ceramic continued

4-in-sq glazed ceramic UA

6-in-sq ceramic TT

3 × 6-in handcrafted, wood-fired glazed ceramics UA

6-in-sq handcrafted, wood-fired glazed ceramic UA

2 × 8-in handmade ceramic UA

4-in-sq crackle-glazed ceramic UA

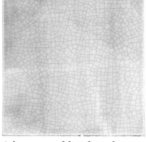

4-in-sq glazed ceramic UA

2 × 8-in ceramic UA

1¾ × 6-in ceramic UA

4-in-sq glazed ceramic UA

6-in-sq handcrafted, wood-fired glazed ceramics UA

8-in-sq glazed ceramic UA

3 × 6-in hand-carved, hand-painted ceramic UA

4 × 6-in handmade glazed ceramic UA

3-in-sq ceramic TT

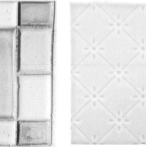

6-in-sq glazed ceramic UA

3 × 6-in glazed-ceramic TT

4-in-sq handmade glazed ceramic UA

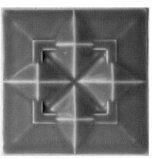

4-in-sq ceramic UA

5½-in-sq glazed ceramic UA

6-in-sq ceuna-style glazed ceramic MT

2 × 8-in-sq glazed ceramic UA

4-in-sq hand-painted glazed ceramic XT

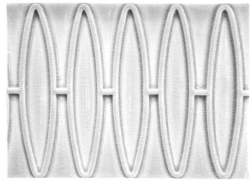

5 × 8-in earthenware AS

4 × 8-in glazed
ceramic SS

3 × 6-in glazed
ceramic HTB

4 × 6-in hand-painted
glazed ceramic XT

4¼-in-sq handcrafted
ceramic AT

6-in-sq bead-board
ceramic AS

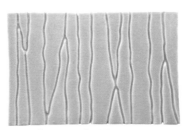

4 × 6-in ceramic AS

8 × 24-in glazed ceramic SS

6 × 15-in glazed ceramic UA

1⅞ × 8-in glazed ceramic UA

2¼ × 8-in glazed ceramic UA

3¼ × 8-in glazed ceramic UA

4½ × 12-in metallic-glazed ceramic UA

4-in-sq hand-painted glazed ceramic XT

30-cm-sq handmade terra-cotta LMM

ceramic continued

4-in-sq handmade ceramics UA

8-in-sq ceuna-style glazed ceramic frieze MT

4 × 6-in glazed ceramic UA

4¼-in-sq and 2⅛-in-sq handcrafted ceramics UA

3½ × 12-in glazed ceramic AT

3 × 6-in handmade ceramic UA

2 × 4-in ceramic UA

2 x 4-in handcrafted glazed stoneware AS

2 × 4-in handcrafted glazed stoneware AS

4 × 6-in handmade ceramic UA

6-in-sq handcrafted ceramic AT

20-cm-sq handmade, hand-painted ceramic DUC

2 × 8-in glazed ceramics AS

4-in-sq ceramic with ¾ × 4-in liner UA

6-in-sq ceuna-style glazed ceramic MT

2 × 8-in handcrafted glazed ceramic AT

2 × 6-in glazed ceramic UA

4 × 6-in handmade glazed ceramic UA

ceramic continued

4-in-sq handcrafted watercolor-glazed ceramic
AT

4¼-in-sq handcrafted ceramic AT

6½-in-sq handcrafted ceramic AT

3 × 6-in beveled
ceramic HTB

3 × 6-in glazed
ceramic HTB

4-in-sq handcrafted
glazed ceramic AT

4¼ × 6½-in handcrafted ceramic AT

4-in-sq handcrafted watercolor-glazed
ceramic AT

4 × 6-in dip-glazed
ceramic MT

6-in-sq hand-painted ceramic AT

4¼-in-sq handcrafted, glazed ceramic AT

2-in-sq handcrafted, glazed ceramic AT

6½-in-sq glazed ceramic AT

4-in-sq handcrafted, glazed ceramic AT

4-in-sq handcrafted ceramic AT

4-in-sq hand-painted ceramic AT

4-in-sq hand-painted ceramic AT

4-in-sq hand-painted ceramic AT

5-in-sq hand-painted ceramic Delftware AT

Multisized hand-painted ceramics UA

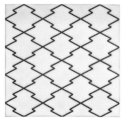

8-in-sq hand-painted stoneware AS

8-in-sq hand-painted stoneware AS

8 × 3-in ceramic AS

8 × 3-in ceramic AS

3 × 6-in beveled glazed stoneware AS

3 × 6-in ceramic AS

5¾ × 7¾-in hand-carved ceramic AS

2½ × 6-in stoneware AS

4-in-sq ceramic AS

2 × 4-in handcrafted glazed stoneware AS

6 × 12-in glazed stoneware AT

4-in-sq ceramic AS

2 × 4-in handcrafted glazed stoneware AS

4-in-sq ceramic AS

2 × 4-in handcrafted glazed stoneware AS

4¼-in-sq ceramic AS

2 × 4-in handcrafted glazed stoneware AS

4-in-sq ceramic AS

2 × 4-in handcrafted glazed stoneware AS

5¾-in-sq ceramic AS

ceramic continued

4¼-in-sq ceramic AS

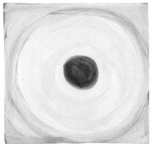

4-in-sq hand-painted
earthenware AS

5¾-in-sq ceramic AS

3¾-in-sq hand-painted,
hand-cut clay-body ceramic
AS

3¾-in-sq hand-painted,
hand-cut clay-body ceramic
AS

3¾-in-sq hand-painted,
hand-cut clay-body ceramic
AS

3¾-in-sq hand-painted,
hand-cut clay-body ceramic
AS

6-in-sq hand-painted earthenware AS

4¼-in-sq ceramic AS

3¾-in-sq hand-painted,
hand-cut clay-body ceramic
AS

6-in-sq ceramic AS

1 × 4¼-in ceramic AS

3 × 6-in ceramic AS

2 × 5-in glazed earthenware AS

4-in-sq limestone-painted stoneware AS

6-in-sq handcrafted glazed ceramic AT

4¼-in-sq ceramic AS

6-in-sq ceramic AS

2 × 5-in hand-painted ceramic AS

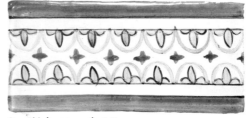

2 × 4¼-in ceramic AS

8-in-sq hand-painted stoneware AS

6-in-sq ceramic AS

2-in-sq ceramic AS

3 × 6-in ceramic AS

4½-in-sq hand-painted
ceramic AS

4½-in-sq hand-painted
ceramic AS

6½-in-diameter ceramic AS

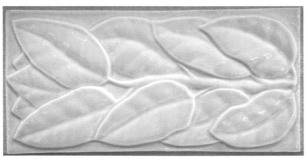

3 × 6-in ceramic AS

3 × 6-in glazed stoneware AS

4-in-sq handcrafted glazed ceramic AT

6-in-sq glazed porcelain AS

6-in-sq handcrafted glazed ceramic AT

3¾-in-sq hand-painted, hand-cut clay-body ceramic AS

6-in-sq bas-relief dip-glazed ceramic MT

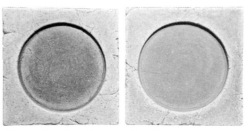

4-in-sq handmade ceramics UA

4-in-sq limestone-painted stoneware AS

2 × 4-in handcrafted glazed stoneware AS

8-in-sq hand-painted stoneware AS

2 × 6-in ceramic AS

2 × 6-in ceramic AS

8-in-sq hand-painted stoneware AS

5-in-sq ceramics HTB

2⅛ × 6-in ceramic AS

5¹⁄₁₀-in-sq delft earthenware MAT

8-in-sq hand-painted stoneware AS

8-in-sq hand-painted stoneware AS

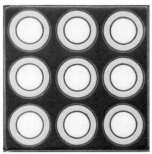

5¾-in-sq ceramic AS

8-in-sq hand-painted stoneware AS

6-in-sq hand-glazed stoneware MOD

8-in-sq hand-painted stoneware AS

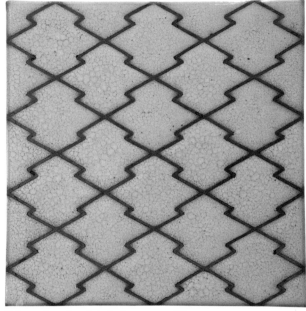

8-in-sq hand-painted stoneware AS

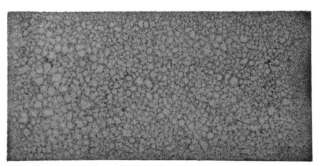

2 × 4-in handcrafted glazed stoneware AS

6-in-sq ceramic AS

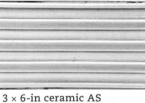

3 × 6-in ceramic AS

2 × 4-in handcrafted glazed stoneware AS

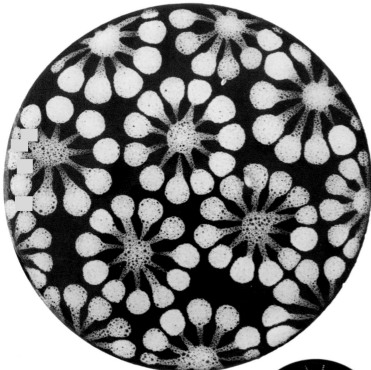

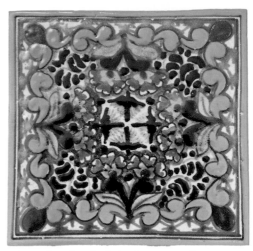

4-in-sq handcrafted Mexican ceramic NT

6-in-diameter hand-painted
glazed ceramic XT

6 × 8-in hand-painted
glazed ceramic XT

4-in-sq handcrafted Mexican ceramic NT

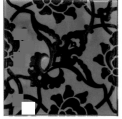

9¼-in-sq handcrafted
quartz-based ceramic
AS

4¾-in-sq quartz Iznik
tile IZ

9¼-in-sq handcrafted quartz-based ceramic
AS

9¼-in-sq handcrafted
quartz-based ceramic
AS

9¼-in-sq handcrafted
quartz-based ceramic
AS

4 × 6-in hand-painted glazed ceramic XT

4-in-sq handcrafted
Mexican ceramic NT

4-in-sq handcrafted
Mexican ceramic NT

8 × 2-in handmade,
glazed ceramic JMS

8 × 2-in handmade,
glazed ceramic JMS

8 × 2-in handmade,
glazed ceramic JMS

8 × 2-in handmade,
glazed ceramic JMS

4-in-sq handcrafted Mexican ceramic NT

3½ × 2-in handmade,
glazed ceramic JMS

3½ × 2-in handmade,
glazed ceramic JMS

3½ × 2-in handmade,
glazed ceramic JMS

1½ × 8-in ceramic AS

3 × 6-in hand-glazed stoneware MOD

3 × 6-in hand-glazed stoneware MOD

4-in-sq handcrafted Mexican ceramic NT

8-in-sq hand-painted
stoneware AS

terra-cotta

8-in-sq terra-cotta TIC

16-in-sq terra-cotta AT

11¼ × 11½-in handmade glazed Moroccan terra-cotta mosaic AS

5⅜ × 11-in handmade glazed Moroccan terra-cotta AS

8-in-sq terra-cotta TIC

4 × 8-in glazed terra-cotta UA

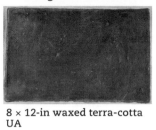

8 × 12-in waxed terra-cotta UA

6¼-in-sq antiqued terra-cotta UA

5¼ × 12⅜-in border and checkerboard mosaic in Moroccan glazed terra-cotta UA

4-in-sq handmade, hand-painted terra-cotta UA

8-in-sq terra-cotta TIC

8-in-sq terra-cotta TIC

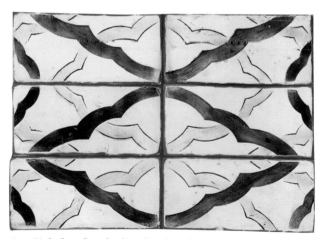

9 × 4¼-in handmade, hand-painted terra-cotta UA

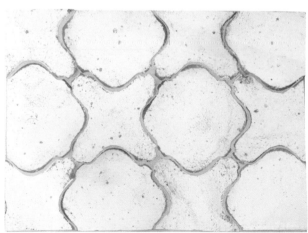

6 × 6¼-in handmade, hand-painted terra-cotta UA

composites

23⅝-in-sq glass agglomerate BI

23⅝-in-sq glass agglomerate BI

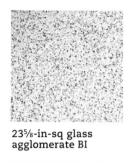

23⅝-in-sq glass
agglomerate BI

23⅝-in glass
agglomerate BI

12-in-sq quartz
composite with
mirror sprinkles SS

12-in-sq quartz
composite with
seashell sprinkles SS

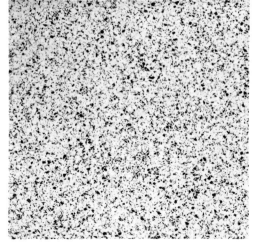

23⅝-in-sq glass agglomerate BI

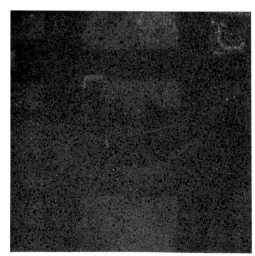

23⅝-in glass agglomerate BI

porcelain

18 × 36-in interconnecting matte-glazed porcelain HTB

12 × 24-in through-body porcelain (detail) NTC

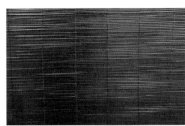

12 × 24-in through-body porcelain (detail) NTC

13-in-sq glazed porcelain DIA

13½ × 22-in glazed porcelain NTC

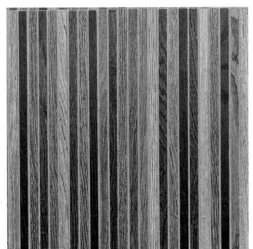

12-in-sq glazed porcelain lamellare mosaic HTB

24-in-sq porcelain (detail) HTB

12-in-sq through-body porcelain (detail) NTC

49-cm-sq rectified through-body porcelain (detail) HTB

49-cm-sq rectified through-body porcelain (detail) HTB

49-cm-sq rectified through-body porcelain (detail) HTB

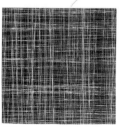

24-in-sq porcelain (detail) HTB

porcelain continued

24-in-sq glazed porcelain (detail) HTB

24-in-sq porcelain (detail) HTB

24-in-sq porcelain (detail) HTB

24-in-sq glazed porcelain (detail) HTB

13-in-sq glazed porcelain (detail) DIA

21-in-sq glazed porcelain with cut corner HTB

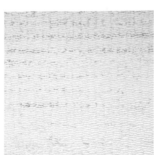

12-in-sq porcelain (detail) HTB

12-in-sq porcelain (detail) HTB

12 × 24-in glazed porcelain LC

12 × 24-in porcelain NTC

4 × 24-in and 6 × 24-in porcelain NTC

24-in-sq glazed porcelain (detail) HTB

$19^5/_8$ × $39^3/_8$-in, $^1/_8$-in-thick through-body porcelain CDC

9 × 35½-in through-body porcelain FIO

60-cm-sq porcelain LC

10-cm-sq through-body porcelain MC

24-in-sq glazed porcelain (detail) HTB

24-in-sq glazed porcelain (detail) HTB

24-in-sq glazed porcelain (detail) HTB

24-in-sq glazed porcelain (detail) HTB

4 × 36-in and 8 × 36-in glazed porcelain HTB

45 × 90-cm glass-inlaid glazed, rectified porcelain MC

32 × 49-cm white-paste bicottura porcelain CAM

32-cm-sq glazed porcelain CC

60-cm-sq porcelain LC

3 × 16-in glazed porcelain HTB

12 × 24-in glazed porcelain LC

8 × 20-in glazed earthenware ABK

porcelain continued

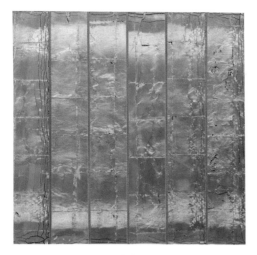

4 × 24-in glazed porcelain RCA

12 × 24-in rectified porcelain COE

16 × 24 in glazed porcelain RCA

24-in-sq glazed porcelain RCA

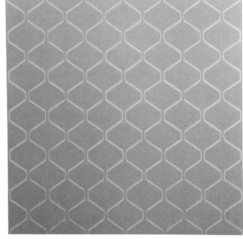

45-cm-sq glazed porcelain LC

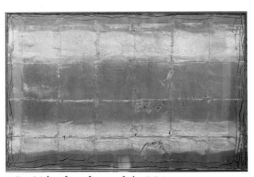

16 × 24 in glazed porcelain RCA

33 × 100-cm porcelain GA

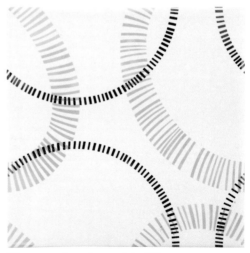

20-cm-sq glazed porcelain CC

20 × 50-cm glazed,
double-fired porcelain
ABK

44-cm-sq glazed porcelain PER

10 × 50-cm glazed,
double-fired porcelain
ABK

32 × 96-cm glazed
porcelain CC

17 × 57-cm porcelain CV

32 × 49-cm white-paste bicottura porcelain CAM

porcelain continued

20-cm-sq white-body ceramic ATL

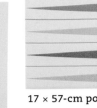

34-cm-sq porcelain CV

17 × 57-cm porcelain CV

17 × 57-cm porcelain CV

3-mm-thick, 50 × 100-cm porcelain CV

32 × 96-cm glazed rectified porcelain SET

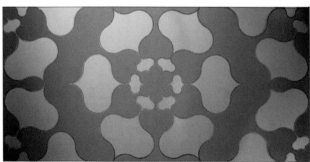

3-mm-thick, 50 × 100-cm porcelain CV

32 × 96-cm glazed rectified porcelain SET

17 × 57-cm porcelain CV

18-in-sq rectified porcelain COE

34-cm-sq porcelain CV

20 × 50-cm glazed, double-fired porcelain ABK

34-cm-sq porcelain CV

32 × 96-cm glazed porcelain SET

24 × 72-cm through-body glazed, rectified porcelain and
3 × 72-cm liner SET

24 × 72-cm through-body glazed porcelain SET

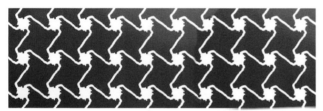

24 × 72-cm through-body glazed porcelain SET

34-cm-sq porcelain CV

 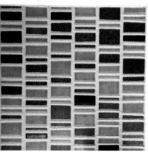

25 × 45-cm glazed porcelain
ATL

30-cm-sq crackle-glazed
raku-effect porcelain
faux-mosaic SET

32 × 96-cm glazed porcelain SET

45 × 90-cm glazed porcelain EG

24-in-sq porcelain PRO

18-in-sq rectified porcelain MC

12-in-sq porcelain AT

24-in-sq porcelain PRO

12-in-sq through-body porcelain SS

12-in-sq porcelain SS

12-in-sq porcelain SS

12-in-sq through-body porcelain SS

24-in-sq through-body porcelain SS

16 × 49-cm white-body porcelain EG

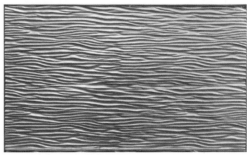

12 × 24-in porcelain PRO

12 × 24-in porcelain PRO

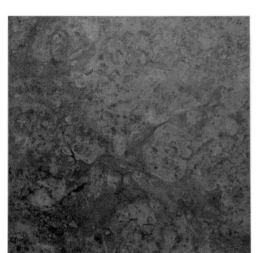

24-in-sq through-body porcelain SS

16-in-sq through-body porcelain SS

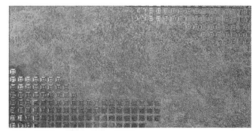

12 × 24-in porcelain PRO

20 × 50-cm porcelain EG

16-in-sq through-body porcelain SS

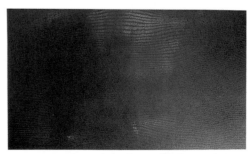

45 × 90-cm through-body rectified porcelain EG

12-in-sq through-body porcelain SS

16-in-sq through-body porcelain SS

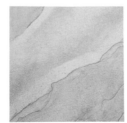

16-in-sq through-body porcelain SS

eco-friendly materials

30-cm-sq bamboo and resin DU

4-in-sq high-fired, custom-glazed, recycled-content ceramic SS

4-in-sq high-fired, custom-glazed recycled-content ceramic SS

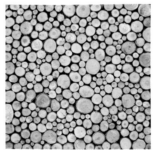

30-cm-sq sliced wood and resin DU

6-in-sq engineered stone with post-industrial recycled glass chips SS

5-in-sq hand-cast, hand-cut recycled molten iridescent glass HTB

6-in-sq engineered stone with post-industrial recycled glass chips SS

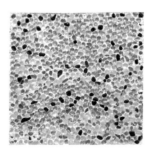

100-percent postconsumer recycled-glass mosaic on 12-in-sq sheets SS

1-in-sq handcrafted ceramic mosaic AT

4-in-sq high-fired, recycled-content ceramic SS

30-cm-sq mother-of-pearl mosaic DU

6-in-sq engineered stone SS

¾-in-sq recycled coconut-shell mosaic on 12-in paper-backed sheets NTC

4-in-sq recycled aluminum EI

4-in-sq high-fired, custom-glazed recycled-content ceramic SS

4-in-sq high-fired, custom-glazed recycled-content ceramic SS

4-in-sq recycled aluminum EI

5 × 10-in hand-cast, hand-cut recycled molten iridescent glass HTB

4-in-sq recycled aluminum EI

2-in-sq hand-cut recycled aluminum mosaic with glass inserts AS

½-in-sq recycled coconut-shell mosaic on 12-in paper-backed sheets NTC

2¼ × 9¾-in hand-cast, hand-cut recycled molten iridescent glass liner OG

6-in-sq engineered stone with post-industrial recycled glass chips SS

6 × 12-in recycled leather UA

14 × 22-in interlocking cork MIO

14 × 22-in interlocking cork MIO

TRIMS

A surprising assortment of specialized trim pieces exists. Peruse slim, sylphlike liners in exotic finishes and rectangular borders traced with scrollwork or Greek key motifs designed to edge a swath of less animated field tile. More exuberant moldings and cornices in ceramic or even leather can re-create the look of traditional woodwork for a more classical result, while inserts of stunning shell or lustrous white bronze can decorate a space like fine jewelry. If you're curious about how such trims are used to compose a refined tile surface, flip to the section entitled "The Little Details," beginning on page 103.

borders and liners

2 × 10-in back-leafed glass mosaic border DB

2 × 10-in back-leafed glass mosaic border DB

2 × 10-in back-leafed glass mosaic border DB

2 × 10-in back-leafed glass mosaic border DB

1⅜ × 6-in ceramic rope border NTC

2½ × 6-in handmade ceramic NTC

1 × 6-in ceramic string-of-pearls border NTC

1⅞ × 9¾-in hand-cast, hand-cut recycled molten glass liner OG

2 × 8-in handmade ceramic NTC

¾ × 12-in bronze trim AT

2 × 8-in handmade ceramic border UA

3 × 12-in etched, stained Jerusalem limestone liner UA

¾ × 6-in etched, stained travertine liner UA

2 × 8-in-sq glazed ceramic liner UA

3¼ × 8-in etched Jerusalem stone border UA

1 × 9-in hand-cast, hand-cut recycled molten iridescent glass liner HTB

2 × 8-in ceramic border UA

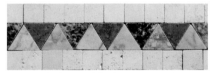

7¼ × 1½-in marble-inset Jerusalem limestone mosaic border NTC

1 × 8-in handmade ceramic border UA

¾ × 8-in faux-painted plaster liner AT

1½ × 8½-in etched, stained travertine liner UA

3¼ × 8¼-in handcrafted ceramic AT

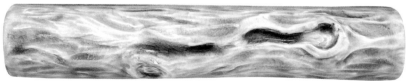

2 × 8-in glazed ceramic UA

1½ × 7½-in handcrafted, glazed ceramic AT

borders and liners continued

5½ × 11-in ceramic border AS

1¾ × 8-in ceramic border AS

2 × 5½-in handcrafted glazed ceramic AT

2 × 8-in-sq glazed ceramic border UA

2 × 8-in ceramic border AS

2 × 8-in-sq glazed ceramic border UA

2 × 8-in earthenware liner AS

3 × 11-in ceramic border AS

1 × 6-in ceramic liner AS

1 × 6-in ceramic trim AS

1¾ × 8-in ceramic border AS

4 × 16-in hand-cut, acid-etched limestone TR

1 × 4⅛-in handmade ceramic border NTC

½ × 9-in etched, stained travertine liner UA

2 × 4¼-in ceramic border AS

1 × 4¾-in handmade ceramic border UA

2¼ × 9½-in hand-cast, hand-cut recycled molten glass liner HTB

3 × 12-in hand-cut, painted limestone TR

2 × 4¼-in ceramic AS

3 × 6-in ceramic border AS

1 × 6-in limestone-painted stoneware half-round AS

1 × 6-in bronze liner AS

2 × 6-in limestone-painted stoneware trim AS

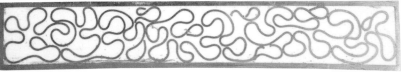

½ × 8-in and ¾ × 8-in handcrafted cast-metal trims AT

2 × 14-in hand-dyed, hand-stamped Herman Oak leather trims AS

4 × 12-in painted limestone UA

1 × 6-in enamel-on-metal cloisonné AS

1¾ × 6-in bronze liner AS

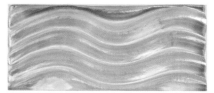

2¾ × 7⅞-in recycled molten glass OG

1 × 6-in limestone-painted stoneware AS

2½ × 8-in glazed earthenware border AS

1¼ × 6-in shell liner UA

1½ × 12-in cast-bronze liner AS

¾ × 6-in and 3 × 6-in glazed ceramics UA

1½ × 11-in ceramic liner AS

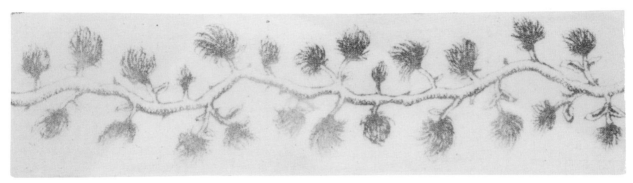

1¾ × 6-in handmade ceramic border UA

8½ × 2-in handcrafted, glazed ceramic AT

1 × 8-in faux-painted plaster liner AT

2½ × 6-in-sq glazed ceramic trim UA

2 × 6-in limestone-painted stoneware trim AS

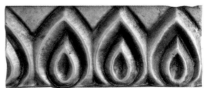

2⅝ × 6¼-in bronze trim AS

corners

20-cm-sq handmade
Moroccan cement PD

2-in-sq brownlip seashell
corner molding UA

Multisized glazed ceramics (20-in-sq detail) AT

8-in-sq terra-cotta TIC

Multisized hand-cut, hand-painted, Aquatina-etched
limestone TR

inserts

2-in-sq handcrafted glazed ceramic AT

1⅞-in-sq ceramic AT

2-in-diameter hand-painted
ceramic mural tiles AT

2-in-sq handcrafted glazed
ceramic AT

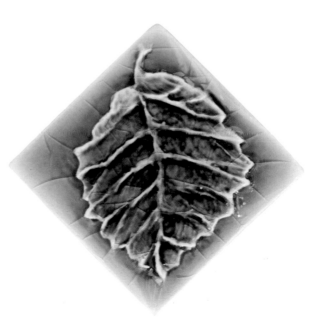

1⅞-in-sq ceramic AT

moldings and cornices

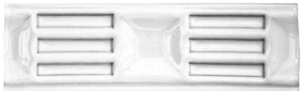

2 × 6-in ceramic cornice HTB

2 × 6-in ceramic cornice UA

2 × 6-in ceramic cornice HTB

6 × 3¾-in glazed ceramic cornice HTB

3 × 6-in ceramic border AS

3 × 6-in ceramic border AS

6 × 3¾-in glazed ceramic cornice HTB

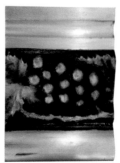
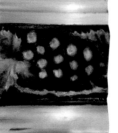

Custom-sized pewter molding (4 × 5½-in detail) UA

14½ × 4-in faux-painted plaster molding AT

3 × 8-in ceramic crown molding AS

3 × 8-in ceramic crown molding AS

4 × 6-in right-end crown molding MT

2½ × 6-in trim AS

3¾ × 8-in earthenware crown molding AS

3½ × 12-in leather molding AS

2 × 8-in ceramic molding UA

Custom-sized pewter molding (4 × 2¾-in detail) UA

2 × 8-in handcrafted, hand-glazed ceramic molding AT

1 × 8-in faux-stone plaster molding AT

6-in-sq handcrafted, wood-fired, glazed-ceramic molding UA

3¾ × 6-in ceramic base AS

3 × 6-in ceramic border AS

7½ × 4-in handcrafted, wood-fired, glazed-ceramic molding UA

2 × 8-in checkerboard shell molding UA

3 × 8-in earthenware chair rail AS

3 × 8-in handcrafted glazed-ceramic molding AT

3 × 6-in ceramic molding AS

2 × 4-in recycled molten glass crown cap OG

COLOR

From vibrant ruby reds to sunshiny yellows, using a brightly hued tile is one of the easiest ways to inject a room with liveliness and joie de vivre. Glazes come in every color of the rainbow, from pastel washes to intensely sultry violets. The following pages also reveal that there's nothing basic about black or white—especially when paired with each other. For tips on using color in your home, turn to chapter 1, "The Big Picture," page 45.

reds

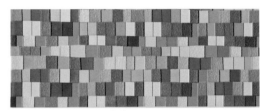

200 × 500-cm porcelain RA

Custom-sized handmade glass mosaic DB

Multisized handmade, hand-cut glass mosaic on 12 × 10½-in sheets TR

20-cm-sq glazed ceramics DEB

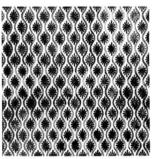

30-cm-sq glazed *terra cotto* MAM

32½ × 65-cm through-body porcelain KR

¾-in-sq paper-backed, recycled coconut-shell mosaics NTC

¼ × 2-in mini-brick glass mosaic NTC

4-in-sq handcrafted ceramic AT

3 × 6-in ceramic subway tile NTC

1½-in-sq hand-crafted, wood-fired glazed ceramics UA

20-cm-sq handmade Moroccan cement PD

4-in-sq hand-formed, glazed ceramic AT

½-in-sq Venetian-enamel glass mosaic BI

6-in-diameter hand-painted glazed ceramic XT

2 × 4-in handcrafted glazed stoneware AS

Custom-sized handmade glass mosaic DB

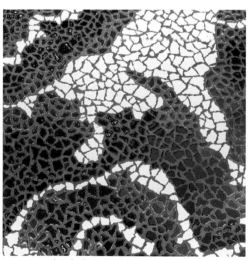

Custom-sized glazed lava rock mosaic AD

yellows and oranges

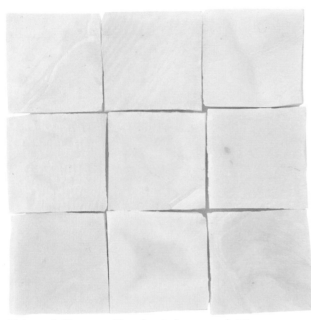

¾-in-sq ladle-poured hand-cut glass mosaic VI

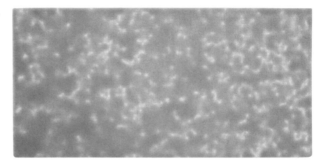

3 × 6-in ceramic UA

3 × 5½-in handcrafted glazed ceramic AT

20-in-sq handmade ceramic CEVI

4-in-sq shattered glass AT

4-in-sq handmade ceramic NTC

3 × 6-in ceramic subway tile NTC

4-in-sq handcrafted glazed ceramic AT

2-in-sq handcrafted ceramic AT

8-in-sq glazed ceramic HTB

4-in-sq shattered glass AT

¾-in-sq glass mosaic BI

4 × 16-in glazed ceramic SS

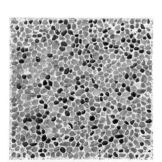
100-percent postconsumer recycled-glass mosaic on 12-in-sq sheets SS

2½ × 10-cm glazed lava rock mosaic on 30-cm-sq sheets AD

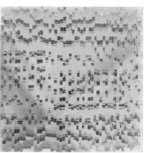
8-in-sq light-conducting acrylic-polymer SEN

4-in-sq hand-formed, glazed ceramic AT

greens

6-in-sq glazed, beveled ceramics ED

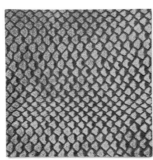

4-in-sq leather EL

¾-in-sq glass mosaic BI

5-in-sq handcrafted glazed ceramic AT

3 × 6-in hand-molded,
tumbled-edge ceramic
subway tile NTC

4¼-in-sq handcrafted
ceramic AT

12-in-sq Aquatina-etched limestone TR

¾-in-sq ladle-poured hand-cut glass mosaic VI

2 × 4-in handcrafted glazed stoneware AS

1½ × 6-in handcrafted glazed ceramic AT

3 × 6-in hand-glazed stoneware MOD

½ × 6-in beveled, glazed ceramic trims ED

Custom-sized handmade glass mosaic DB

4-in-sq hand-formed, glazed ceramic AT

4-in-sq hand-formed, glazed ceramic AT

blues

6-in-sq glazed beveled ceramics ED

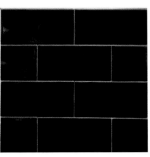

3 × 6-in ceramic subway tile NTC

4-in-sq handmade ceramic relief NTC

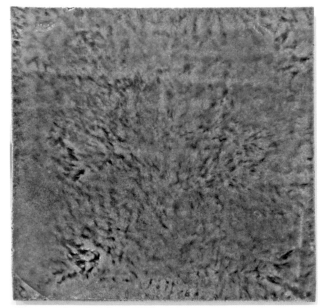

40-cm-sq handmade ceramic CEVI

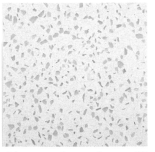

6-in-sq engineered stone SS

4¼-in-sq handcrafted ceramic AT

6-in-sq ceuna-style glazed ceramic MT

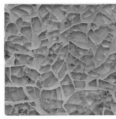

¾-in-sq glass mosaic BI

4-in-sq shattered glass AT

4-in-sq handcrafted ceramic AT

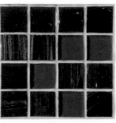

4-in-sq handcrafted, glazed ceramic AT

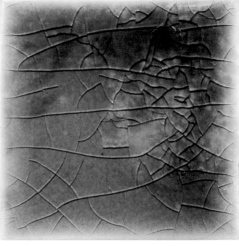

4-in-sq handcrafted Victorian-glazed ceramic AT

4-in-sq handcrafted glazed ceramic AT

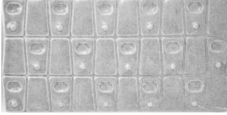

3 × 6-in hand-glazed stoneware MOD

¼ × 2-in mini-brick glass mosaic NTC

4-in-sq handcrafted ceramic AT

4-in-sq handcrafted glazed ceramic AT

4-in-sq glass TR

4-in-sq recycled-content high-fired ceramic SS

2 × 4-in handcrafted glazed stoneware AS

2 × 4-in handcrafted glazed stoneware AS

pinks and purples

20-cm-sq glazed porcelain CC

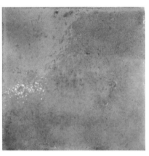

20-cm-sq handmade terra-cotta LMM

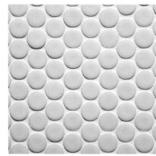

¾-in-diameter glazed ceramic penny rounds UA

1 × 6-in handmade glazed ceramics UA

Custom-sized handmade glass mosaic DB

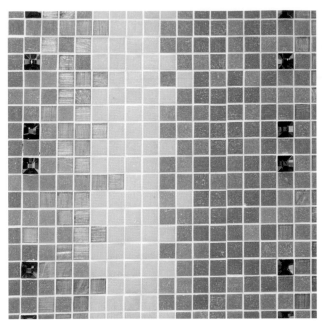

¾-in-sq glass mosaic with custom Swarovski Strass crystal inserts TR

6½ × 40-cm glazed lavastone MAM

5-in-sq handcrafted glazed ceramic AT

4-in-sq handcrafted glazed ceramic AT

¾-in-sq glass mosaic BI

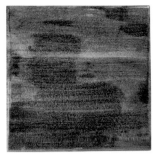

20-cm-sq handmade ceramic CEVI

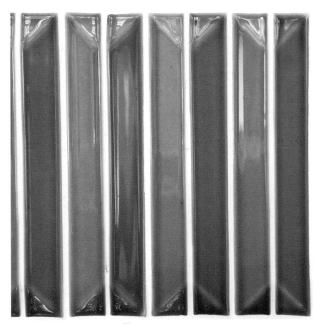

½ × 6-in beveled glazed ceramic trims ED

⅜-in-sq glass mosaic BI

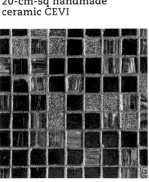

¾-in-sq glass mosaic BI

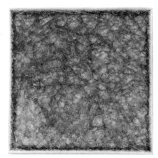

4-in-sq handcrafted glazed ceramic AT

vivids

12 × 24-cm glazed porcelain LC

33 × 50-cm porcelain CC

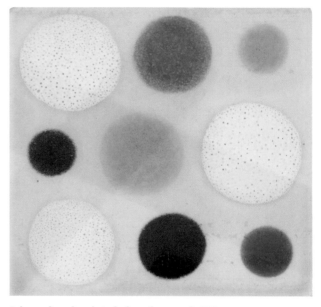

4-in-sq hand-painted glazed ceramic XT

1⅜ × 6-in ceramic borders NTC

½-in-sq netted high-fired ceramic mosaics NTC

6-in-sq glazed, beveled ceramics with 1-in-sq ceramic trims ED

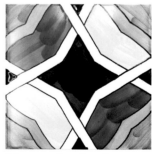

20-cm-sq handmade ceramic CEVI

20 × 100-cm hand-painted, glazed ceramic BAR

4 × 6-in handcrafted ceramic AT

15 × 15-cm handcrafted cotto SLN

20-cm-sq handmade terra-cotta LMM

4-in-sq handcrafted watercolor-glazed ceramic AT

4 × 10-in hand-painted glazed ceramic XT

9¼-in-sq handcrafted ceramic AS

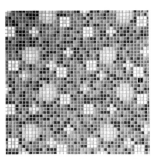

½-in-sq Venetian-enamel glass mosaic BI

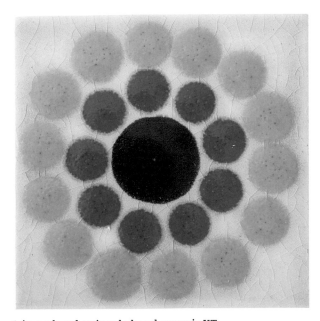

4-in-sq hand-painted glazed ceramic XT

9¼-in-sq handcrafted ceramic AS

4-in-sq acid-etched, metal-leafed Brazilian natural-cleft slate AT

pastels

Custom-sized handmade glass mosaic DB

4-in-sq handcrafted ceramic
AT

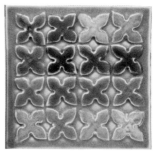

4-in-sq handcrafted
watercolor-glazed ceramic
AT

2 × 4-in etched glass NTC

1¹/₂ × 6-in and 2 × 6-in
handmade ceramics UA

3 × 6-in beveled ceramic HTB

4-in-sq beaded ceramic AS

4-in-sq hand-formed, glazed ceramic AT

4-in-sq handcrafted glazed ceramic AT

4-in-sq handcrafted, hand-glazed ceramic AT

6-in-sq hand-painted ceramic UA

12-in-sq painted limestone UA

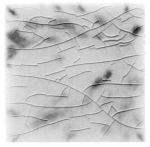

4-in-sq handcrafted Victorian-glazed ceramic AT

4-in-sq handcrafted ceramic AT

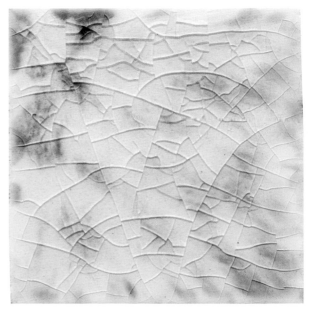

4-in-sq handcrafted Victorian-glazed ceramic AT

¾-in-sq glass mosaic BI

4-in-sq handcrafted watercolor-glazed ceramic AT

whites

6-in-sq hand-glazed stoneware MOD

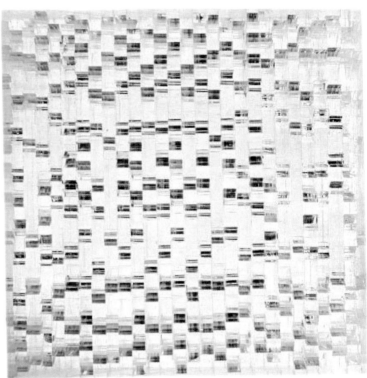

8-in-sq light-conducting acrylic-polymer SEN

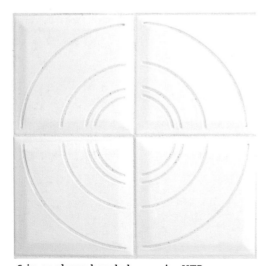

6-in-sq glossy beveled ceramics HTB

3 × 6-in handcrafted ceramic AT

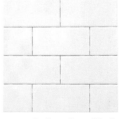

3 × 6-in hand-molded, tumbled-edge ceramic NTC

3 × 6-in ceramic AS

10-in-sq ceramic AS

3 × 6-in hand-glazed stoneware MOD

2 × 6-in handcrafted ceramic AT

3 × 6-in ceramic subway
tile UA

3 × 6-in glazed ceramics UA

4¼-in-sq handcrafted
ceramic AT

4-in-sq glazed earthenware
AS

4¼-in ceramic UA

3¾ × 6-in ceramic UA

4-in-sq glazed ceramic UA

3-in-sq ceramics UA

2 × 6-in ceramic HTB

3½ × 8-in handcrafted ceramic AT

6-in-sq handcrafted ceramic AT

3 × 8-in glazed ceramic UA

3¾ × 8-in handcrafted ceramic AT

2 × 6-in handcrafted ceramic AT

1-in-sq glazed beveled ceramics ED

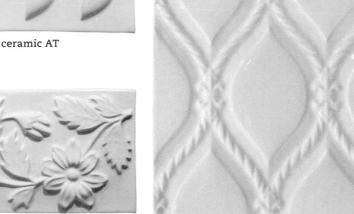

6-in-sq handcrafted ceramic AT

6-in-sq handcrafted, glazed ceramic UA

2 × 6-in handcrafted ceramic AT

2 × 6-in handcrafted ceramic AT

2 × 6-in handcrafted ceramic AT

blacks

8-in-sq hand-painted stoneware AS

3 × 9-in handcrafted stoneware AS

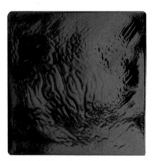

4-in-sq hand-cast, hand-cut recycled molten glass OG

24-in-sq porcelain (detail) HTB

4⅛-in-sq handmade ceramic NTC

1-in-sq glazed beveled ceramics ED

6-in-sq beveled ceramic HTB

¾-in-sq ladle-poured hand-cut glass mosaic VI

4-in-sq leather EL

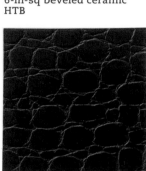

4-in-sq leather EL

12 × 24-in through-body colored porcelain (detail) NTC

16 × 24-in glazed porcelain RCA

45-cm-sq glazed porcelain LC

3 × 6-in hand-glazed stoneware MOD

4-in-sq hand-formed, glazed ceramic AT

TEXTURE

Find out how even the slightest variations in surface texture can make a huge difference in the look of a certain material—or an entire room. A wall of rough-hewn stacked stone lends a space earthy appeal while a three-dimensional run of faceted, glossy glass squares invites frequent caresses. A motif such as basket weave or stripes raised slightly above the surrounding surface imparts an intriguing tactility, as does an embossed pattern mimicking woven textiles. For more tricks on how texture can affect the vibe of a space, see chapter 1, "Designing with Tile," page 55.

dimensional

2 × 4-in ceramics UA

10-cm-sq beveled hand-painted ceramic mosaics KR

4-in-sq ceramic UA

4-in-sq handmade ceramic NTC

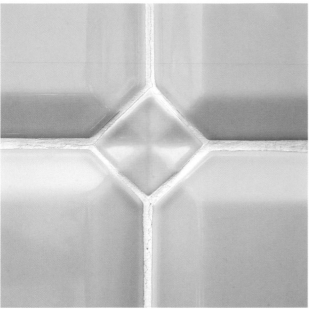

1-in-sq glazed beveled ceramic trim ED

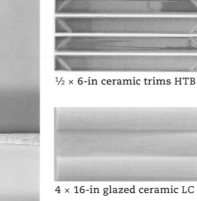

½ × 6-in ceramic trims HTB

4 × 16-in glazed ceramic LC

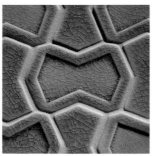

4 × 8-in beveled-edge glazed ceramic TT

3 × 6-in beveled ceramic HTB

3 × 6-in glazed beveled ceramics ED

4 × 24-in sandstone UA

1³⁄₁₆-in-sq through-body porcelain mosaic MC

Multisized glazed ceramic mosaic WZ

4 × 16-in glazed ceramic LC

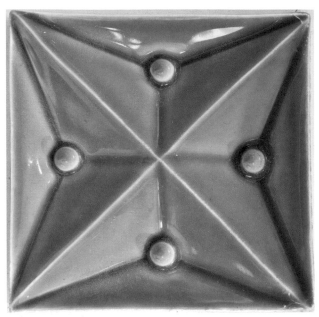

4-in-sq ceramic AS

2-in-sq handcrafted ceramic AT

2-in-sq handcrafted ceramic AT

4-in-sq handcrafted ceramic AT

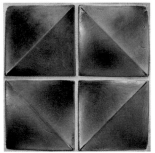

3-in-sq handmade recycled-content glass AS

6-in-sq ceramic AS

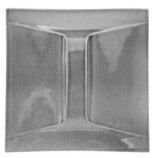

6-in hand-glazed stoneware MOD

6-in-sq hand-glazed stoneware MOD

3½ × 6-in ceramic AS

4-in-sq ceramic AT

4-in-sq ceramic AT

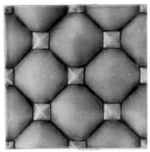

6-in-sq handcrafted cast metal AT

4-in-sq handcrafted ceramic AT

6-in-sq hand-glazed stoneware MOD

4-in-sq limestone-painted stoneware AS

6-in-sq ceramic AS

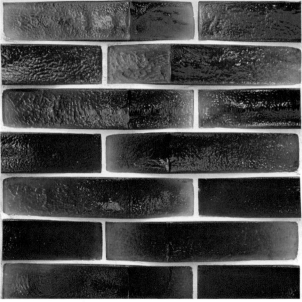

2 × 9-in handmade recycled-content glass relief tiles with hand-broken edge AS

4-in-sq ceramic AS

2 × 8-in convex ceramics NTC

relief

4-in-sq metallic glass AT

3¾-in-sq glazed ceramic AT

30-cm-sq cement agglomerate CDC

4-in-sq metallic glass AT

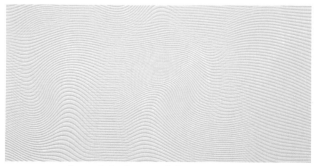

30 × 60-cm through-body porcelain MA

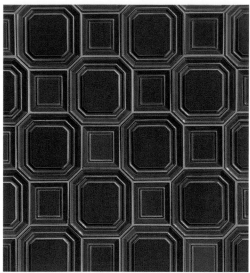

16-in-sq glazed ceramic WZ

12½-in-sq ceramic HTB

3 × 8-in glazed ceramic UA

3 × 8-in glazed ceramic UA

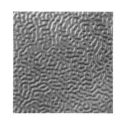

20-cm-sq porcelain FG

4 × 16-in glazed ceramic LC

4 × 16-in glazed ceramic LC

3 × 6-in ceramic border UA

4 × 16-in glazed ceramic LC

4 × 6-in handcrafted ceramic AT

4 × 7½-in-sq glazed ceramic border UA

4 × 6-in handmade ceramic UA

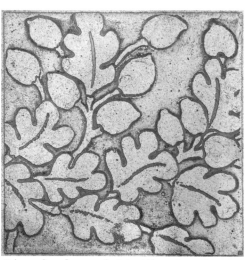

6-in-sq hand-carved etched limestone UA

4-in-sq earthenware AS

6-in-sq handcrafted, wood-fired glazed ceramic UA

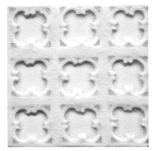

4-in-sq glazed ceramic UA

6-in-sq handcrafted, hand-glazed ceramic AT

4-in-sq ceramic AT

6-in-sq handcrafted ceramic AT

4¼-in-sq handcrafted ceramic AT

2 × 4-in stoneware AS

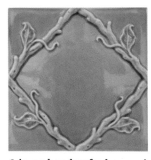

6-in-sq handcrafted ceramic AT

6-in-sq handcrafted ceramic AT

6-in-sq handcrafted ceramic AT

4-in-sq stoneware AS

4¼-in-sq ceramic AS

4-in-sq stoneware AS

4¼-in-sq handcrafted ceramic AT

8 × 9-in handcrafted, wood-fired ceramic panel UA

4 × 8-in earthenware AS

3¼ × 8¼-in handcrafted ceramic AT

4 × 6-in ceramic AT

subtle

6-in-sq handcrafted ceramic
AT

6-in-sq Amarello and Crema
Marfil mosaic, tumbled UA

6-in-sq Amarello and Crema
Marfil mosaic, chiseled UA

3 × 6-in, 3-in, and 1½ × 6-in handmade ceramics UA

6-in-sq Amarello and
Crema Marfil mosaic,
polished UA

6-in-sq Amarello and Crema
Marfil mosaic, water-jet cut
UA

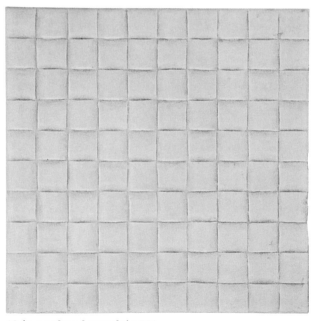

12-in-sq porcelain SS

18-in-sq rectified porcelain
MC

13-in-sq glazed porcelain DIA

2-in-sq etched limestone mosaic NTC

6 × 8-in micro-line-chiseled Novela Crème SS

4 × 6-in ceramic AS

4 × 8-in hammer-textured ceramic UA

12 × 24-in through-body colored porcelain NTC

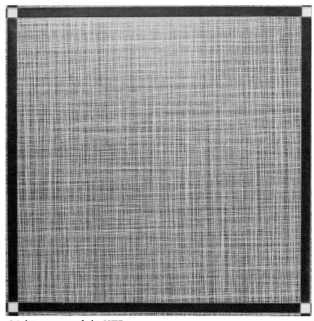

24-in-sq porcelain HTB

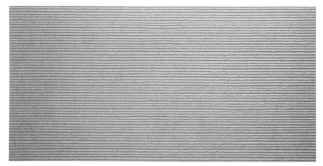

12 × 24-in porcelain SS

MURALS, FRIEZES, AND COMPOSITIONS

Talk about power in numbers: Many tiles feature imaginative patterns—lyrical cherry blossoms, nautical scenes—designed to be installed in series to form a pictorial composition. Great for backsplashes and recessed niches, or to embellish a swath of more neutral tile, these creative murals become works of art.

14-in-sq ceramic medallion AS

5¾-in hand-painted, hand-cut clay-body medallion AS

4-in-sq glazed ceramics UA

6-in-sq glazed ceramics with 1 × 8-in borders AT

20-cm-sq handmade Moroccan cement PD

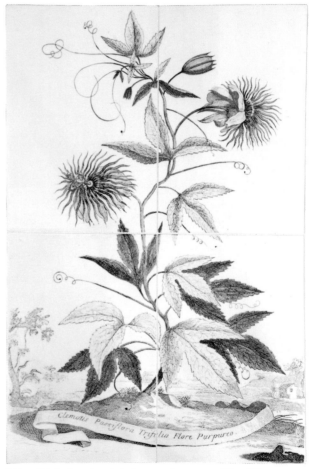

9½ × 6¼-in hand-painted ceramic composition UA

8-in-sq hand-painted stoneware mural AS

12 × 18-in pressed, glazed stoneware UA

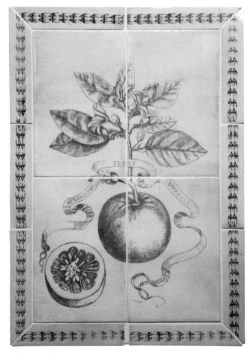

9¾ × 14¾-in hand-painted ceramics;
1⅛ × 6½-in hand-painted borders UA

4-in-sq glazed
earthenware AS

20-cm-sq handmade
Moroccan cement PD

6-in-sq limestone-
painted stoneware AS

murals, friezes, and compositions continued

5-in-sq hand-painted
ceramic delftware AT

4-in-sq hand-painted
glazed ceramics XT

20-in-sq glazed-ceramic composition AT

7½ × 23-in slip-trail-
glazed ceramic mural
TT

6-in-sq glazed
ceramics UA

6-in-sq ceramics AS

8-in-sq ceramics HTB

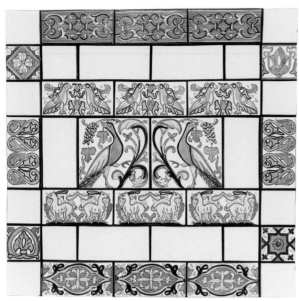

18-in-sq handmade ceramic NTC

4⅛-in-sq handmade ceramics NTC

5-in-sq ceramics HTB

6-in-sq ceramics AS

8-in-sq ceramics HTB

20 × 100-cm hand-painted glazed ceramics BAR

4⅛-in-sq handmade ceramics NTC

5-in-sq hand-painted ceramic delftware AT

MOTIFS

For a kid's room, a backsplash, or an aquatic-themed beach house, pick tile to reflect and reinforce the surrounding décor. Choose whimsical designs embellished with hand-painted images of kittens, fresh fruit, or delftware sailboat scenes. Whether your taste runs to traditional fleurs-de-lis or prancing monkeys, there's a tile to suit your style.

animals

6-in-sq hand-painted ceramic AT

4 × 6-in handcrafted watercolor-glazed ceramic AT

3¾-in-sq glazed ceramic hooks AT

4-in-sq handmade glazed ceramic UA

1 × 8-in handcrafted watercolor-glazed ceramic AT

4⅛-in-sq handmade ceramics NTC

4⅛-in-sq handmade ceramic NTC

4⅛-in-sq handmade ceramic with 2-in-sq insert NTC

4 × 8-in handcrafted watercolor-glazed ceramic AT

animals continued

6-in-sq hand-sculpted, hand-pressed stoneware AT

4½-in-sq hand-painted ceramic AS

4⅛-in-sq handmade ceramic NTC

6-in-sq hand-sculpted, hand-pressed stoneware AT

3 × 6-in glazed ceramic TT

6-in-sq handmade ceramic UA

4⅛-in-sq handmade ceramic NTC

birds and insects

5-in-sq hand-painted ceramic Delftware AT

8-in-sq ceramic HTB

8-in-sq ceramic HTB

8-in-sq ceramic HTB

8-in-sq ceramic HTB

4⅛-in-sq handmade ceramic NTC

8-in-sq hand-painted stoneware AS

8-in-sq ceramic HTB

20-cm-sq handmade terra-cotta LMM

5-in-sq hand-painted
ceramic Delftware AT

4⅛-in-sq handmade
ceramic NTC

20-cm-sq handmade, hand-painted ceramic
DUC

5-in-sq ceramic HTB

4-in-sq handcrafted
glazed ceramic AT

3-in-sq handcrafted glazed
ceramic AT

4-in-sq handcrafted glazed
ceramic AT

30-cm-sq handmade, hand-
painted ceramic DUC

8-in-sq ceramic HTB

5¼-in-sq ceramic MAT

6 × 8-in hand-painted
glazed ceramic XT

4 × 6-in hand-painted
glazed ceramic XT

4 × 5¾-in etched travertine UA

6-in-sq glazed ceramic UA

nautical

4-in-sq handcrafted watercolor-glazed ceramic AT

4-in-sq handcrafted watercolor-glazed ceramic AT

4-in-sq handcrafted watercolor-glazed ceramic AT

5-in-sq hand-painted ceramic delftware AT

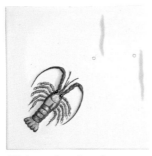

4⅛-in-sq handmade ceramic NTC

4⅛-in-sq handmade ceramic NTC

4 × 8-in handcrafted watercolor-glazed ceramic AT

4 × 8-in handcrafted watercolor-glazed ceramic AT

2 × 4-in handcrafted watercolor-glazed
ceramic AT

2 × 6-in hand-carved ceramic AS

4¼-in-sq ceramic AS

2 × 8-in handcrafted watercolor-glazed ceramic AT

4⅛-in-sq handmade ceramic NTC

4 × 8-in handcrafted watercolor-glazed ceramic AT

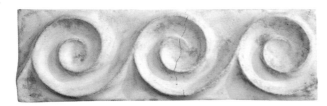

2 × 6-in limestone-painted stoneware AS

4⅛-in-sq handmade ceramic NTC

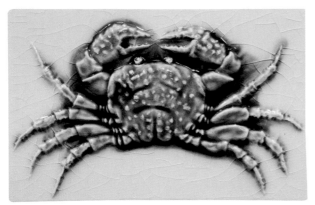

6 × 4-in handcrafted watercolor-glazed ceramic AT

4-in-sq handcrafted watercolor-glazed ceramic AT

4¼-in-sq handcrafted ceramic AT

4¼-in-sq ceramic AS

14½ × 4-in handcrafted ceramic AT

5-in-sq hand-painted ceramic delftware AT

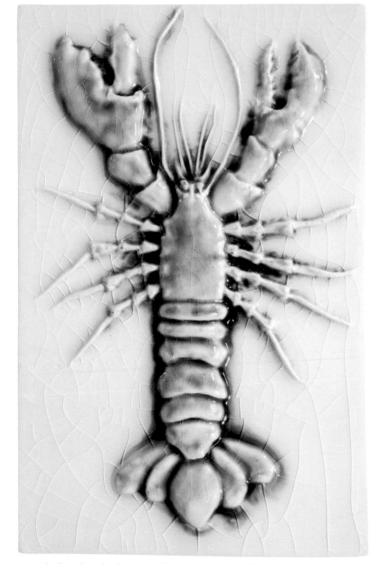

4 × 6-in handcrafted watercolor-glazed ceramic AT

3 × 6-in handmade glazed ceramic UA

5¹⁄₁₀-in-sq delft earthenware MAT

plants and flowers

2 × 4¼-in ceramic border AS

4-in-sq hand-painted glazed ceramic XT

4⅛-in-sq handmade ceramic NTC

8-in-sq ceramic HTB

8-in-sq ceramic HTB

8-in-sq ceramic HTB

4¼-in-sq handcrafted
ceramic AT

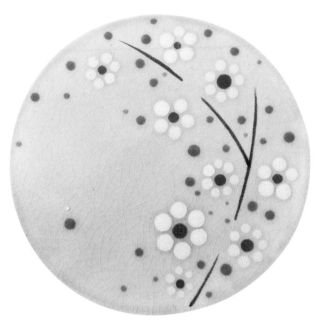

6-in-diameter hand-painted glazed ceramic XT

4-in-sq ceramic NTC

8-in-sq hand-painted
stoneware AS

30-cm-sq glazed *terra cotto* MAM

6-in-sq etched, stained
Jerusalem limestone UA

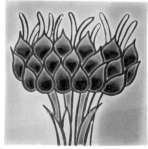

4-in-sq hand-painted glazed
ceramic XT

1¾ × 5¾-in hand-painted, hand-cut clay-body liner AS

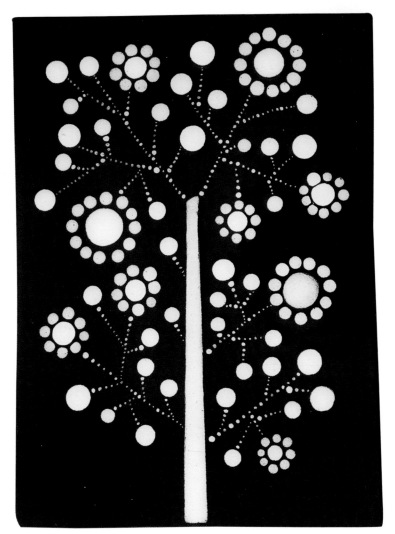

7½ × 10½-in hand-painted glazed ceramic XT

3½-in-sq etched, stained travertine UA

3½-in-sq etched,
stained travertine UA

4-in-sq glazed
ceramic UA

8-in-sq ceramic HTB

4½-in-sq hand-painted
ceramic AS

2-in-sq glazed ceramic AT

6-in-sq hand-painted ceramic AT

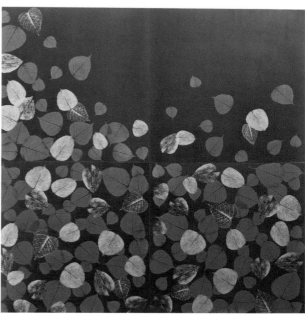

24-in-sq porcelain PRO

3-in-sq ceramic AS

6-in-sq etched, stained
dark Travertine UA

4-in-sq hand-painted glazed ceramic XT

12 × 24-in rectified
porcelain COE

food and cooking

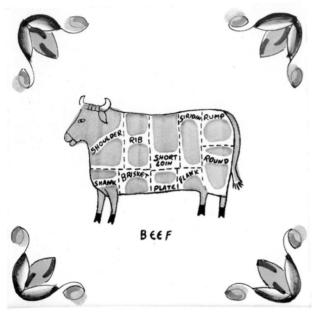

4⅛-in-sq handmade ceramic NTC

4½-in-sq hand-painted
ceramic AS

4⅛-in-sq handmade
ceramic NTC

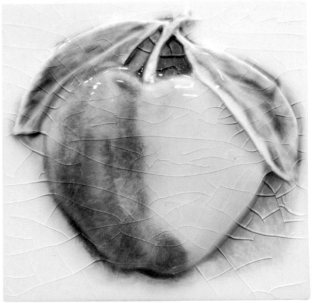

4-in-sq handcrafted watercolor-glazed ceramic
AT

12 × 16-in glazed ceramic AT

2 × 4-in
handcrafted
ceramic AT

6-in-sq hand-painted ceramic AT

4-in-sq glazed ceramic NTC

4-in-sq handcrafted glazed ceramic AT

6-in-sq hand-painted ceramic AT

4-in-sq handcrafted Mexican ceramic NT

6-in-sq hand-painted ceramic AT

4⅛-in-sq glazed ceramic NTC

fleurs de lis

8-in-sq terra-cotta
TIC

3½-in-sq etched,
stained travertine UA

6-in-sq ceramic AS

10 × 10-cm hand-
crafted *cotto* SLN

20-cm-sq handmade, hand-painted ceramic AD

6-in-sq glazed
ceramic UA

1½ × 6¾-in handmade ceramic UA

4-in-sq ceramic AT

2 × 4¼-in ceramic AS

3 × 6-in etched
travertine UA

6-in-sq etched,
stained dark
travertine UA

6-in-sq Jerusalem gold and Nero Marquina
mosaic with 1 × 6-in white Thassos marble
border NTC

PATTERN

You'll no doubt be inspired after seeing the myriad tile patterns at your disposal, from fashion-forward textile-inspired motifs like houndstooth and toile to damask prints reminiscent of wallpaper. Go boldly graphic with geometric shapes, or stay subtle with a surface designed to look like leather or crocodile skin. Read more about how to add panache with pattern by turning to "Pattern and Shape," page 51.

damask, toile, and brocade

8 × 16-in glazed porcelain HTB

19⅝-in × 39⅜-in, ⅛-in-thick through-body porcelain CDC

12 × 24-in glazed porcelain LC

boxes

12-in-sq back-leafed
glass mosaics DB

6-in-sq beveled
ceramics HTB

30-cm lavastone MAM

3-in-sq ceramics TT

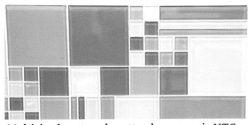

5 x 8-in glazed earthenware AS

30-cm-sq crackle-glazed raku-effect porcelain
faux-mosaic SET

3⅞-in-sq handcrafted,
wood-fired glazed
ceramics UA

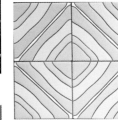

5¾-in-sq ceramics AS

2-in-sq handcrafted
glazed ceramic AT

8-in-sq handmade
cement UA

Multisized textured matte glass mosaic NTC

3 × 6-in glazed, beveled ceramics ED

loops, ribbons, and curves

20 × 60-cm glazed ceramic DEB

34-cm-sq porcelain CV

60-cm-sq glazed porcelain LC

16 × 32½-in rectified porcelain FIO

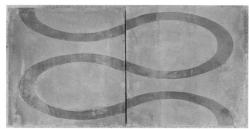

20-cm-sq handmade Moroccan cement PD

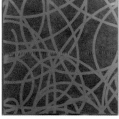

45-cm-sq glazed porcelain LC

12-in-sq water-jet-cut Thassos marble mosaic AT

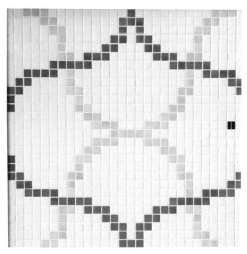

¾-in-sq glass mosaic BI

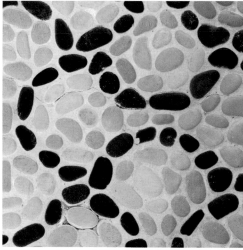

Random-sized pebble mosaics with 14-in-sq repeat UA

geometrics

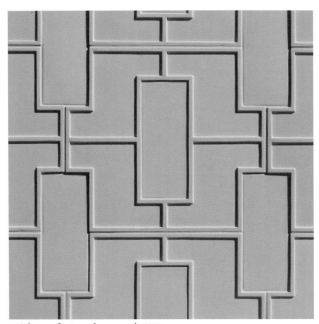

16-in-sq fretwork ceramic WZ

Custom-sized handmade
back-leafed glass mosaic DB

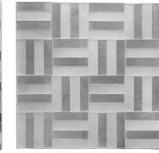

12-in-sq back-leafed glass
mosaics DB

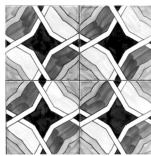

20-in-sq handmade
ceramics CEVI

Custom-sized back-leafed
glass mosaic DB

3 × 6-in, 1 × 6-in, and 2 × 4-
in Alba Chira mosaic NTC

8 × 2-in and 3½ × 2-in
handmade, glazed ceramics
JMS

10 × 10-cm handcrafted
cotto SLN

5¾-in-sq glazed ceramic AS

12 × 13⅞-in hexagonal concrete AS

20-in-sq handmade ceramics CEVI

20-in-sq handmade ceramics CEVI

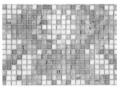

17 × 57-cm porcelain CV

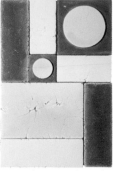

4 × 6-in, 2 × 6-in, 2-in, and 4⅛-in handmade ceramics UA

4½-in-sq ceramic AS

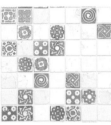

1-in-sq embossed Biancone mosaics COT

⅜-in-sq glass mosaic (detail) BI

Multisized handmade, hand-cut glass mosaic TR

4⅛-in-sq handmade ceramic NTC

8-in-sq ceramic (detail) HTB

4⅛-in-sq handmade ceramic NTC

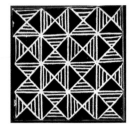

4⅛-in-sq handmade ceramic NTC

4¼ × 9¼-in handcrafted ceramic AT

5-in-sq glazed ceramic HTB

geometric continued

½-in-sq Venetian-enamel glass mosaic BI

¾-in-sq glass mosaic BI

5 × 7-in handmade ceramics AT

2-in-sq handcrafted glazed ceramic AT

4⅛-in-sq handmade ceramic NTC

12-in-sq hand-inlaid 12-in-sq paper-backed metal with 6-in repeat MR

Calacatta Gold, Jerusalem gold, and Lagos Azul mosaic with 12-in repeat AT

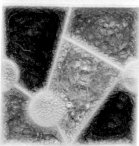

3-in-sq glass-fused ceramics TT

30-cm-sq glazed porcelain LC

8-in-sq hand-painted stoneware AS

7-cm-sq honed Carrera hex with polished Bardiglio and Lettuce Ming mosaic UA

4-in-sq handcrafted ceramic AT

herringbone, houndstooth, and zigzags

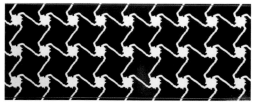

24 × 72-cm through-body glazed porcelain SET

20-cm-sq handmade Moroccan cement PD

20-cm-sq handmade Moroccan cement PD

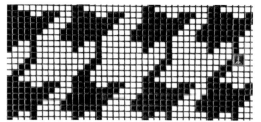

½-in-sq Venetian-enamel glass mosaic (detail) BI

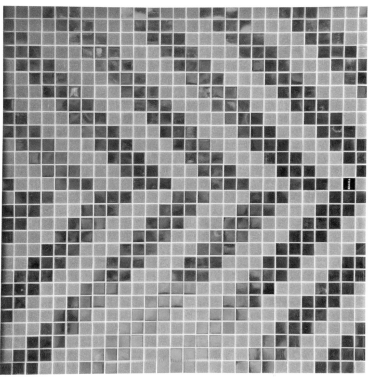

¾-in-sq glass mosaic BI

1 × 3-in Honey onyx mosaic NTC

6½ × 40-cm glazed lavastone MAM

2 × 8-in Lagos Azul with White Carrera marble NTC

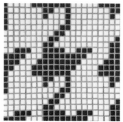

½-in-sq Venetian-enamel glass mosaic (detail) BI

circles, dots, and ovals

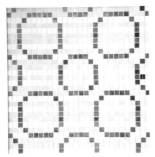

¾-in-sq glass mosaic BI

20-cm-sq handmade terra-cotta LMM

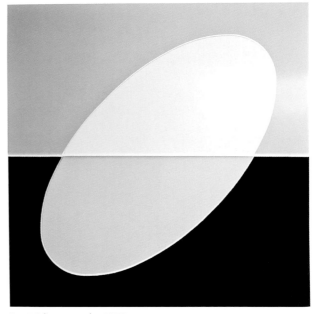

8 × 16-in ceramics HTB

8-in-sq hand-painted stoneware AS

8-in-sq hand-painted stoneware AS

7¾-in-sq ceramic AS

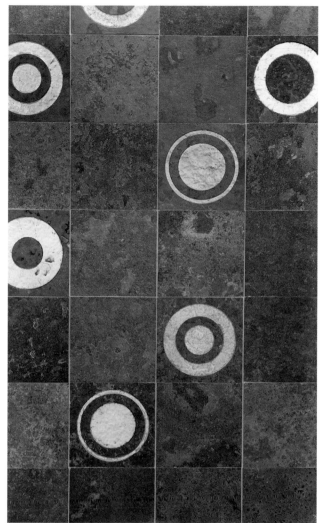

4-in-sq acid-etched, metal-leafed Brazilian natural-cleft slate AT

6-in-sq extruded ceramic CDC

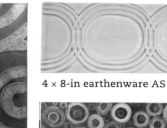

4 × 8-in earthenware AS

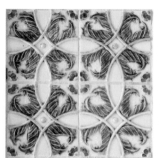

2½ × 7¾-in bamboo and resin AT

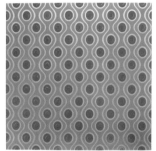

45-in-sq glazed porcelain ECT

6-in-sq glazed ceramics AT

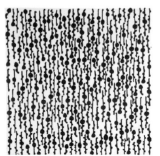

30-cm glazed *terra cotto* MAM

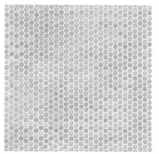

30-cm glazed *terra cotto* MAM

30-cm glazed *terra cotto* MAM

florals

6-in-sq ceuna-style glazed ceramics MT

32 × 49-cm white-paste bicottura porcelain CAM

32 × 96-cm glazed porcelain CC

15-cm-sq glazed *terra cotto* MAM

20 × 50-cm glazed, double-fired porcelain ABK

Custom-sized etched glass (20-in-sq detail) AT

33 × 50-cm glazed porcelain CC

8 × 24-in porcelain HTB

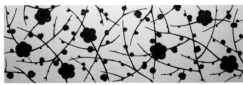

32 × 96-cm glazed rectified porcelain SET

8 × 16-in porcelain
HTB

15-cm-sq glazed *terra cotto* MAM

60-sm-sq handmade ceramic PC

4-in-sq handcrafted ceramic AT

30-cm-sq glazed *terra cotto* MAM

46 × 10-cm porcelain MAR

20 × 50-cm glazed, double-fired porcelain ABK

6-in-sq ceramics AS

plaid and basket weave

1¼ × 2½-in Calacatta marble and ⅝-in Durango mosaic NTC

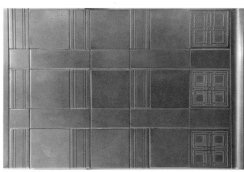

3-in-sq and 1½ × 3-in stainless steel UA

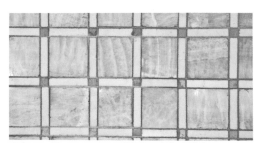

4-in-sq Honey onyx with 1 × 4-in White Thassos strips NTC

Custom-sized handmade, recycled-content glass smalti and 24-karat gold mosaic TR

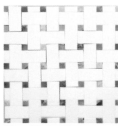

1¼ × 2½-in Logos Azul mosaic NTC

¼ × 2½-in Thassos marble mosaic NTC

2-in-sq, 1-in-sq, and 1 × 2-in handmade glazed-ceramic mosaics TT

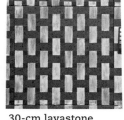

30-cm lavastone MAM

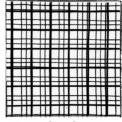

15-cm glazed *terra cotto* MAM

Crema Marfil, Noce travertine, and dark Emperador marble mosaic on 14-in sheets NTC

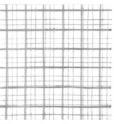

15-cm glazed *terra cotto* MAM

skins and hides

½-in-sq Venetian-enamel
glass mosaic BI

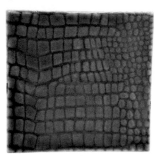

4⅛-in-sq handmade
ceramic NTC

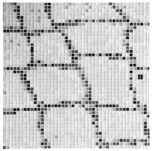

½-in-sq Venetian-enamel
glass mosaic BI

24 × 72-cm porcelain SET

24 × 60-cm glazed ceramics VAL

4-in-sq leather EL

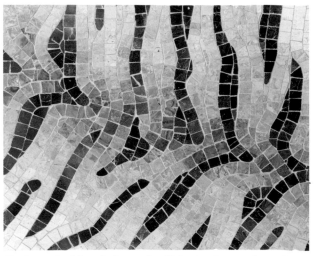

Custom-sized hand-chopped polished red onyx, Jerusalem
gold, gold travertine, and Gialo Realle mosaic UA

SHAPE

A grid of tile is a timeless classic, but why not think outside the box? Diamonds and triangles, circles and squares, interlocking geometries and curve-edged polygons—these are just some of the manifold options to choose from. A shapely installation is guaranteed to turn heads and tickle your fancy.

4-in-sq glazed earthenware AS

4-in-sq glazed earthenware AS

2 × 6-in pressed-relief glazed earthenware AS

2 × 6-in pressed-relief glazed earthenware AS

Multisized glass mosaic NTC

18 × 30-cm handcrafted lava SLN

2½-in-sq glazed ceramic AT

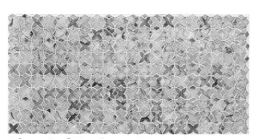

Multisized glass mosaic NTC

4 × 4-in terra-cotta TIC

1-in-sq Azul Macuba marble mosaic TAN

40 × 70-cm handcrafted *cotto* SLN

3 × 4-in terra-cotta TIC

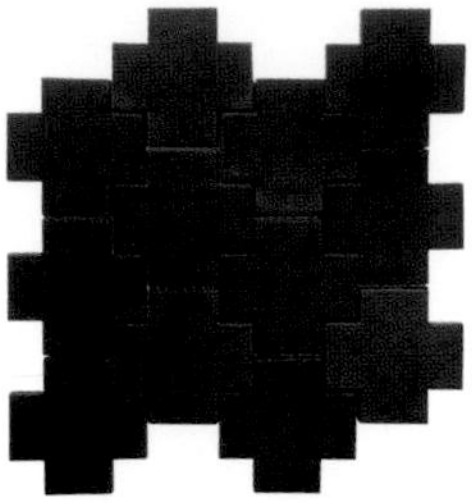

3⅞ × 3⅞-in and
1⅞-in-sq extruded
porcelain CDC

4 × 7-in handcrafted ceramic AT

6 × 6-cm porcelain mosaic COE

3⅞ × 3⅞-in and
1⅞-in-sq extruded
porcelain CDC

4 × 7-in handcrafted ceramic AT

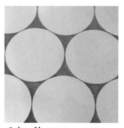

6-in-diameter matte-
glazed ceramics DE

3 × 3-in handcrafted
glazed ceramic AT

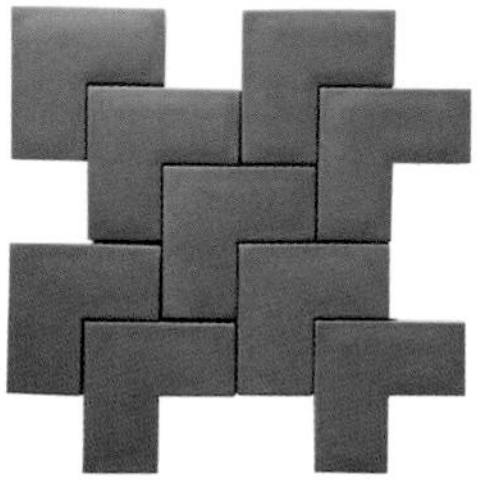

3⅞ × 3⅞-in extruded
porcelain CDC

3 × 5-in handcrafted
glazed ceramic AT

4-in-diameter handcrafted, hand-glazed
ceramic AT

2-in-sq handmade
glazed-ceramic hex
mosaics TT

3 × 3-in handcrafted
glazed ceramic AT

2½ × 6½-in
handcrafted glazed
ceramic AT

2½ × 6-in handcrafted
glazed ceramic AT

4 × 12-in handmade glazed ceramics TT

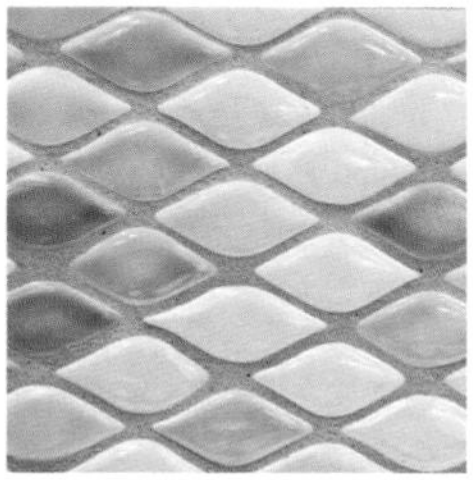

½ × 1-in glazed
ceramic mosaic AT

3 × 3-in handcrafted
glazed ceramic AT

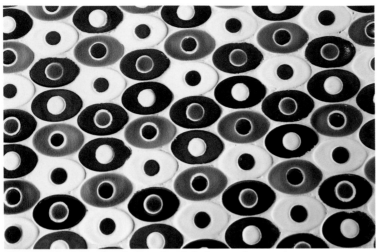

8 × 3-in ceramic AS

8 × 3-in ceramic AS

Custom-sized handmade, hand-painted ceramic mosaic on 9½ × 11-in sheets TR

4 × 8-in pillowed ceramic with ¾-in-sq inserts UA

Custom, multisized glass mosaic (20-in detail) AT

3½ × 5½-in ceramic AT

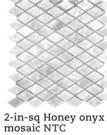

2-in-sq Honey onyx mosaic NTC

2 × 2-in glazed-ceramic hex mosaic AS

2 × 2-in handcrafted glazed ceramics AT

4-in-sq pillowed, glazed porcelain with ⅝-in glazed porcelain gumdrop AS

2 × 5-in glazed earthenware AS

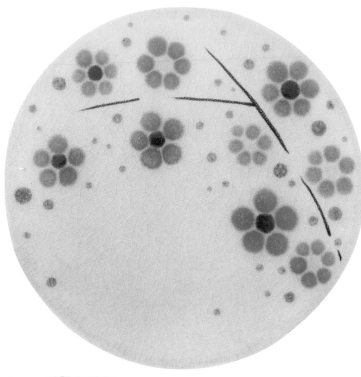

6-in-diameter hand-painted glazed ceramic XT

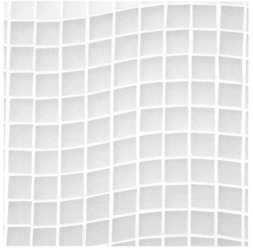

1 × 1-in satin-finished glass mosaic SS

3½ × 3½-in hand-crafted ceramic AT

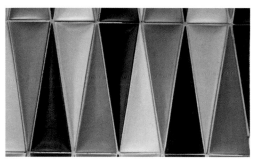

3 × 9-in glazed stoneware AS

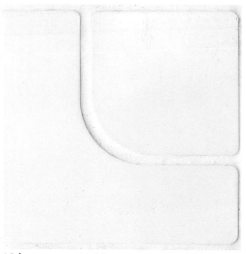

4 × 4-in beveled ceramic HTB

2½ × 8-in ceramic AS

6-in-sq ceramic HTB

16-in-sq concrete AS

shape continued

3 × 3½-in bronze AT

8¼-in-sq molded ceramics UA

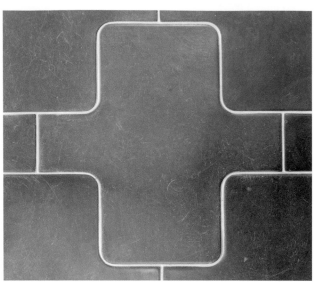

15¾-in-sq concrete AS

8-in-sq handcrafted ceramic AS

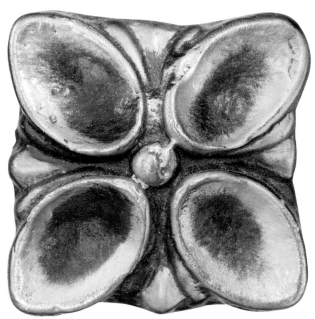

2-in-sq bronze AS

3¼-in-diameter solid-bronze insert AT

15 × 15-cm handcrafted cotto SLN

4 × 7½-in ceramic AS

3 × 5¼-in ceramic AS

3 × 4-in hand-cut glass mosaic on 14-in sheets AS

18-in-sq glazed porcelain NO

5 × 7-in handmade ceramic AT

13 × 13-cm handcrafted *cotto* SLN

6½ × 6½-in ceramic AS

6 × 6-in ceramic AS

3¾ × 3¾-in glazed ceramic with ¾ × 6-in glazed ceramic trim AT

MOSAICS

A technique first practiced in ancient Rome, mosaic artistry has a venerable history. Many modern-day practitioners honor this illustrious tradition with classically inspired designs such as interlacing vines and intricate geometries rendered in minute fragments of exotic marble or onyx. But an explosion of innovative contemporary designs proves equally alluring, using unusual materials like coconut or creating wild prints like leopard spots and romantic roses in full bloom.

12-in repeat back-leafed glass mosaic DB

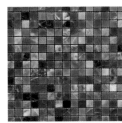

¾-in-sq blue onyx mosaic NTC

¾-in-sq onyx mosaic NTC

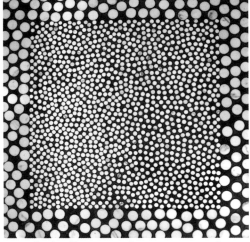

1- and 2-in-diameter Calacatta Oro mosaic NTC

Custom-sized back-leafed glass mosaic DB

Custom-sized back-leafed glass mosaic DB

½-in-sq high-fired ceramic mosaic NTC

30-cm-sq ceramic mosaic with 1-cm engraved dots TRE

½-in-sq ceramic
mosaic NTC

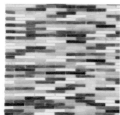

¼ × 2-in minibrick
glass mosaic NTC

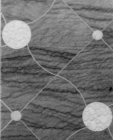

2½ × 12-in liner and
12-in-sq water-jet-cut
mosaic in Calacatta
Oro, Bianco Carrera,
Blue Celeste, Blue
Macuba, White
Thassos UA

12 × 23-in glazed porcelain lamellare mosaic
HTB

½-in-sq ceramic mosaic NTC

¾-in-sq glass mosaic
on 12-in-sq sheets
HTB

¾-in-sq glass mosaic
on 12-in-sq sheets
HTB

¾-in-sq glass mosaic
on 12-in-sq sheets
HTB

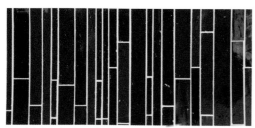

Multisized glass brick mosaic on 12-in sheets
NTC

1-in-sq Jerusalem
limestone mosaic
NTC

2½ × 1⅓-in Jerusalem
limestone brick
mosaic NTC

Bianco Carrera, Nero Marquina, light and dark Emperador marble,
Amarellia, and Crema Marfil marble mosaic with 14-in-sq repeat UA

mosaics continued

Custom-sized handmade glass mosaic DB

Custom-sized handmade glass mosaic DB

Multisized dark and light Emperador marble, Durango, and Carrara marble mosaic NTC

1-in-diameter mother-of-pearl penny mosaic TAN

1-in-sq hand-cast recycled molten glass mosaic OG

¾ × 8-in stoneware mosaic AT

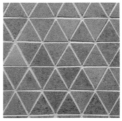

6 × 6-cm porcelain mosaic COE

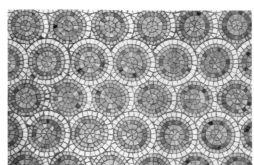

Custom Thassos marble, Blue Macuba, Brecchia, and Celeste mosaic with 9-in repeat UA

Multisized Travertine Noce, light and dark Emperador, and Saint Laurent stick mosaic UA

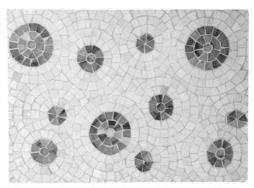

Blue Macuba and polished White Travertino marble mosaic (12 × 16½-in detail) UA

⅜-in-sq glass mosaic BI

⅜-in-sq glass mosaic BI

⅜-in-sq glass mosaic BI

¾-in-sq glass mosaic
BI

⅜-in-sq glass mosaic
BI

1 × 4-in herringbone
Blue Celeste mosaic
NTC

1-in-sq ceramic
mosaic NTC

⅝-in-sq Bianco Feather and Milky Pink mosaic with 13½-in repeat UA

Calacatta marble and Chinese
black mosaic (12 × 18-in detail) UA

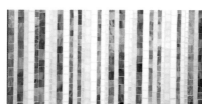

10½ × 20-in glass mosaic AT

9½ × 20-in glass mosaic AT

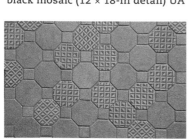

30 × 30-cm glazed porcelain RA

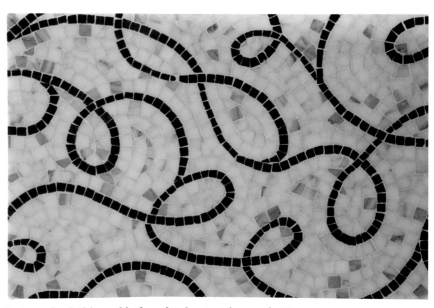

Custom-sized Chinese black and Calacatta Tia mosaic UA

mosaics continued

1-in-sq Pietra Mediterranea limestone in honed and spiaggia finish with glass inserts TR

1-in-sq handcrafted-ceramic mosaic AT

1-in-sq handcrafted, glazed ceramic mosaic (loose or netted) AT

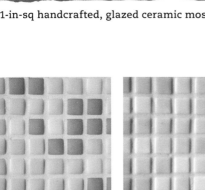

½-in-sq Venetian-enamel glass mosaic BI

½-in-sq Venetian-enamel glass mosaic BI

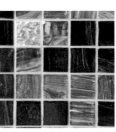

¾-in-sq glass mosaic BI

Custom-sized Jerusalem gold, Thassos marble, and Azul Cielo mosaic with 12-in repeat AT

½-in-sq Venetian-enamel glass mosaic BI

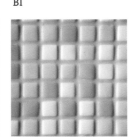

½-in-sq Venetian-enamel glass mosaic BI

¾-in-sq glass mosaic BI

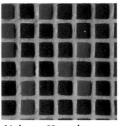

½-in-sq Venetian-enamel glass mosaic BI

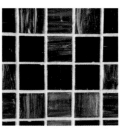

¾-in-sq glass mosaic BI

¾-in-sq ladle-poured, hand-cut glass mosaic VI

¾-in-sq ladle-poured, hand-cut glass mosaic VI

3-in-sq glazed ceramic TT

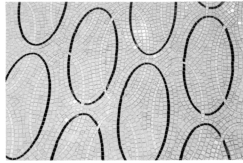

Crema Marfil, Thassos, and miro-mosaic on 12 × 13-in sheets AT

⅜-in-sq glass mosaic BI

3 × 6-in glass mosaic TR

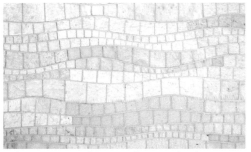

Ming Green marble mosaic on 12-in sheet AT

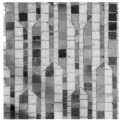

Custom-sized Cipollino and Calacatta Oro marble mosaic UA

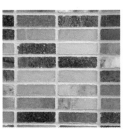

Custom-sized Cipollino marble mosaic UA

½-in-sq Venetian-enamel glass mosaic BI

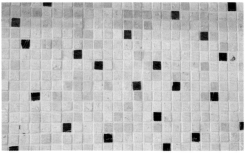

⅝-in-sq limestone mosaic with glass inset TR

Multisized Honey onyx mosaic on 12-in sheets AT

⅝ × 1¼-in honed Inca Gray mosaic on 12-in-sq sheets SS

⅝ × 1¼-in polished Tundra Gray mosaic on 12-in-sq sheets SS

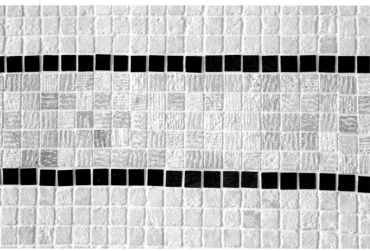

1-in-sq Pietra Mediterranean limestone in honed and spiaggia finish with glass mosaic TR

2-in-diameter hand-cut glass mosaic on 14-in sheets AS

Multisized 1-in-diameter to 4-in-diameter hand-cut glass mosaic on 14-in sheets AS

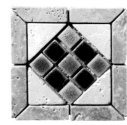

4-in-sq travertine mosaic with high-fired ceramic inserts NTC

⅜-in handcrafted ceramic mosaics SS

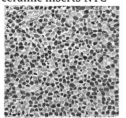

100-percent post-consumer recycled-glass mosaic on 12-in-sq sheets SS

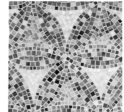

Glass mosaic on 14-in-sq sheets AS

Custom-sized Calacatta Tia and verde luna mosaic with 7½ × 5-in leaf detail UA

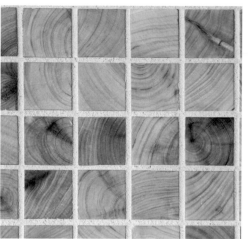

½-in-sq cross-cut honey pine mosaic AT

1-in-sq handcrafted, glazed ceramic mosaic (loose or netted) AT

Hand-chopped tumbled Dark Emperador and white Travertine mosaic with 11 × 13-in repeat UA

Multisized hand-laid river rock mosaic NTC

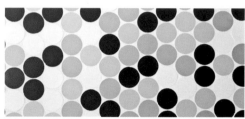

Matte-glazed ceramic penny mosaic on 8 × 16-in sheets HTB

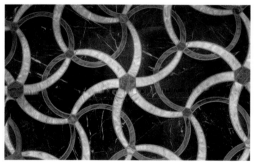

Water-jet-cut mosaic in gold brown, dark onyx, Blue Macuba, and Biano Feat with 20-in-sq repeat UA

Multisized hand-crafted ceramic mosaic SS

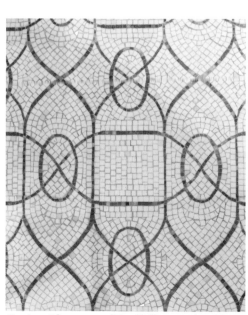

2 × 2-in glazed-ceramic hex mosaic AS

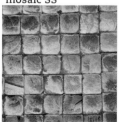

¾-in-sq recycled coconut shell mosaic NTC

Custom Thassos and Bardiglio mosaic with 15 × 19-in repeat UA

12 × 7¾-in etched-travertine border and
½-in-sq travertine mosaic UA

⅝-in-sq and ⅝ × 2-in
limestone mosaic
with ⅝-in-sq glass
inset TR

16 × 26-in honed Calacatta Oro and Montauk
Black water-jet-cut mosaic UA

12-in-sq Indigo
granite, Sky Blue, dark
Bardiglio, and white
Thassos mosaic with
6-in repeat AS

1-in-sq polished onyx mosaic with 2 × 6-in
shell liner UA

4-in slate mosaic AT

1 × 4-in web-backed
soapstone mosaic TU

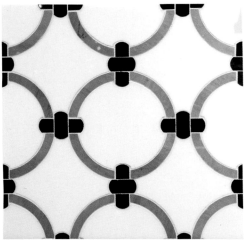

Pietre Dura–style mosaic in Thassos, Bardiglio,
and Negro Marquina with 7-in repeat AS

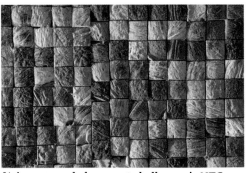

¾-in-sq recycled coconut shell mosaic NTC

Resources

ARCHITECTS AND DESIGNERS

Below is contact and credit information for the designers of the homes featured within these pages.

Troy Adams Design
Pacific Design Center
8687 Melrose Avenue, Suite G292
West Hollywood, CA 90069
310-657-1400
troyadamsdesign.com
Page 80 (cork: Natural Cork)

Jeff Andrews Design
354 W Avenue, Suite 42
Los Angeles, CA 90065
323-227-9777
jeffandrews-design.com
Pages 34–35 (backsplash tile: Bisazza)
Page 130 (wall, floor tile: Walker Zanger)

Juan Carlos Arcila-Duque
4925 Collins Avenue, Suite 10G
Miami Beach, FL 33140
305-604-5828
arcila-duque.com
Pages 66, 116 (reproduction encaustic tiles: Euramex, Inc.)
Pages 9, 23, 24–25, 61 (limestone: Estefano Reiser Floors)

Peter S. Balsam Associates Interior Design
Associates: Peter S. Balsam and Jayne Goldstein
1601 Third Avenue, Suite 20K
New York, NY 10128
212-831-6556
peterbalsam.com
Page 74 (backsplash: Artistic Tile)
Page 125 (floor mosaic: Artistic Tile; wall stone: Artistic Tile)
Page 26 (glass wall and floor tiles: Artistic Tile)

James Chuda, Environmental Architect
310-403-6785
Page 80 (cork floor tile: Natural Cork)
Page 98 (mosaic: Oceanside Glasstile)
Page 98 (glass mosaic, recycled aluminum tile: Classic Tile & Mosaic)
Page 84 (recycled aluminum tile: Classic Tile & Mosaic)

Dale Cohen Design Studio
212-374-9087
dalecohendesignstudio.com
Pages 108–109 (wall tile: Stone Source; trim tile: Ann Sacks; mosaic: New Ravenna Mosaics)

Leo A. Daly
3390 Mary Street, Suite 216
Miami, FL 33133
305-461-9480
leoadaly.com
Page 62 (floor, wall tiles: Roca)

Vanessa Deleon Associates
934½ River Road
Edgewater, NJ 07020
201-224-9060
vanessadeleon.com
Page 11 (dining room wall mosaic: Bisazza)
Pages 12, 102 (bathroom wall tile: Venezia from Porcelanosa; marble floor and wall tile: Artistic Tile)
Page 50 (backsplash: Pratt & Larson through Artistic Tile)

René González Architect
670 NE 50th Terrace
Miami, FL 33137
305-762-5895
renegonzalezarchitect.com
Page 115 (pool tile: Bisazza)

S. Russell Groves
210 Eleventh Avenue, Suite 502
New York, NY 10011
212-929-5221
srussellgroves.com
Page 49 (floor, wall stone: Walker Zanger)
Pages 48–49 (subway tile: Walker Zanger)
Page 82 (wall tile: Globus Cork)

Fanny Haim & Associates
21338 West Dixie Highway
North Miami Beach, FL 33180
305-937-0815
fannyhaim.com
Page 70 (mosaic: Antico Stone)

Jeff Miller Design
302 Elizabeth Street, Suite 4
New York, NY 10012
212-366-1638
jeffmillerdesign.com
Page 112 (wall, floor tile: Stone Source)

Bob Niles
Page 67 (backsplash tile: Avalon Carpet & Tile)
Page 115 (pool tile: Avalon Carpet & Tile)
Page 56 (floor tile: Avalon Carpet & Tile)

One Design + Build
Designer: Hugo Mijares
3436 North Miami Avenue, Suite 1
Miami, FL 33127
786-364-4675
onedbmiami.com
Page 21 (wall tile: Trend)

Pentagram
Partner: James Biber
204 Fifth Avenue
New York, NY 10010
212-683-7000
pentagram.com
Pages 90, 120 (Wall tile: Elgin Butler)
Page 98 (Cork floor tile: Expanko)
Page 92 (Terrazzo pavers: Durite)
Pages 36, 38–39 (floor tiles: custom through Hastings Tile & Bath)

Nicole Sassaman Designs
23852 Pacific Coast Highway,
Suite 621
Malibu, CA 90265
310-457-6120
nicolesassaman.com
Page 54 (shower, wall, floor, and
ceiling tile: Walker Zanger)
Page 118 (fireplace tile: Walker
Zanger)
Page 33 (niche tile: Walker Zanger)

Shields & Company Interiors
Principal: Gail Shields-Miller
149 Madison Avenue, Suite 201
New York, NY 10016
212-679-9130
shieldsinteriors.com
Pages 18, 27 (floor tile: Town &
Country Flooring)
Page 50 (wall tile, mosaic: Town &
Country Flooring)
Page 125 (shower tile, marble
mosaic: Town & Country Flooring)

2Michaels
Principals: Jayne and Joan Michaels
360 Central Park West, Suite 16H
New York, NY 10025
212-662-5359
2michaelsdesign.com
Page 64 (backsplash tile: Heath
Ceramics)

Larry Weinberg
360 Central Park West, Suite 16H
New York, NY 10025
917-861-3574
4pmny.com
Pages 36, 38–39 (floor tiles: custom
through Hastings Tile & Bath)

XO Design Group
3886 Biscayne Boulevard
Miami, FL 33137
305-576-5501
xodesigngroup.de
Page 81 (cork flooring: The Kitchen
and Bath Source.)

CATALOG SHOPPING GUIDE

For ease of reference, each
caption in "The Options"
includes a supplier code in
red type that corresponds to
the credited showroom or
manufacturer listed below.

**ABK Group Industrie Ceramiche
ABK**
Via San Lorenzo 24/A
Finale Emilia, Italy 41034
011-39 0535 761311
abk.it
Decorative glazed porcelain.

Ann Sacks AS
37 East 18th Street
New York, NY 10003
212-529-2800
800-278-8453
Eighteen additional locations
throughout the country; visit the
website for showroom and dealer
locator.
annsacks.com
*A stunning selection of decorative
options including ceramic, leather, glass,
stone, and wood.*

Antiqva Domvs AD
C da. Piraino Pozzillo
S. Caterine Villarmosa, Italy 93018
011-39-0934-672744
antiqvadomvs.it
*Handmade majolica, ceramic, and
terra-cotta tiles with rich glazes.*

Artistic Tile AT
38 West 21st Street
New York, NY 10010
212-727-9331
877-528-5401
Additional locations in White
Plains, New York; Paramus, New
Jersey; and Shrewsbury, New
Jersey.
artistictile.com
*Luxury showroom specializing in exotic
stones and decorative tiles in myriad
materials.*

Bi Marmi MAR
Via Prussiano 50-56
Bisceglie, Italy 70052
011-80-3951389
bimarmi.it
*Classic and contemporary decorative
tile and marble.*

Bisazza BI
43 Greene Street
New York, NY 10013
212-334-7130
800-247-2992
Additional locations in Miami
and Los Angeles.
bisazza.com
*Monochromatic and wallpaper-style
glass mosaics plus an assortment of
large-format glass and terrazzo tiles.*

Casa Dolce Casa CDC
155 Bluegrass Avenue Parkway
Alpharetta, GA 30005
678-393-8050
casadolcecasa.it
*A leader in high-style decorative
ceramics, including superthin and
wallpaper-patterned porcelain and
intriguing shapes.*

Ceramica Bardelli BAR
Via Giovanni Pascoli 4/6
Vittuone, Italy 20010
011-39-02-9025181
bardelli.it
*An Italian ceramics company with a
long history of collaborating with iconic
designers such as Gio Ponti and Piero
Fornasetti.*

Ceramica Campani CAM
Via Radici in Piano 675
Sassuolo, Italy 41049
011-39-0536-816100
ceramicacampani.com
*Inventive ceramic and glazed porcelain
in stonelike patterns.*

Ceramica di Treviso TRE
Via Amendola 1
Villorba, Italy 31050
011-39-04220-608-500
ceramicaditreviso.it
Novel ceramics and mosaics.

Ceramica Fioranese FIO
Via Cameazzo 25
Fiorano Modenese, Italy 41042
011-39-0536-993511
fioranese.it
Porcelain floor and wall tiles ranging from timeless classics to on-trend looks.

Ceramica Viva CV
Via per Sassuolo 70/A
Formigine, Modena, Italy 41043
011-39-0536-998-750
cerviva.it
Ceramic tiles in fun shapes and colors with pop-art appeal.

Cerámicas Diago DIA
Patrida Benadressa sin
Castellón, Spain 12006
011-964-340-717
diago.com
A broad range of ceramic styles.

Ceramiche Atlas Concorde ATL
Atlas Concorde USA
2830 SW 42nd Street
Hollywood, FL 33312
954-791-3066
atlasconcorde.it
A wide range of ceramic and porcelain in pop-art patterns and bold colors.

Ceramiche Coem COE
Via Cameazzo 25
Fiorano Modenese, Italy 41042
011-39-0536-993511
coem.it
A wide selection of ceramic and glazed porcelain.

Ceramiche Provenza PRO
Via 2 Giugno 13/15
Spezzano, Italy 41040
011-39-0536-927611
ceramicheprovenza.com
Fashion-inspired porcelain and other mod contemporary offerings.

Ceramiche Settecento Valtresinaro SET
Via del Crociale 21
Fiorano Modenese, Italy 41042
011-39-0536-928711
settecento.com
Mosaics and ceramics incorporating intriguing textures and damask patterns.

CE.VI Ceramica Vietrese CEVI
Via Gaudio Maiori 71
Cava De' Tirreni, Italy 84013
011-39-089-463933
ceramicacevi.it
Hand-painted ceramic in mesmerizing glazes and lively graphics.

Cerim Ceramiche CC
Via Canaletto 24
Fiorano Modenese, Italy 41042
011-39-0536-840111
cerim.it
Chic wall tiles in glazed porcelain.

Costello Studio, Inc. CS
21-07 41st Avenue, 4th Floor
Long Island City, NY 11101
718-383-8108
csidesigns.net
Custom tooled-leather tiles.

Cotto Veneto COT
Vicolo Tentori 12
Carbonera, Italy 31030
011-39-0422-4458
cottoveneto.it
High-performance glazed ceramic and porcelain.

Dan Bleier Studio DB
236 West 26th Street, Loft 1001
New York, NY 10001
212-255-7019
danbleierstudio.com
Decorative resin wall tiles and handmade glass mosaics with metal-leaf backing.

Decoratori Bassanesi DEB
Via Vallina Orticella 48
Borso Del Grappa, Italy 31030
011-39-0423-910076
decoratoribassanesi.it
Modern interpretations of classic motifs, from florals to geometrics.

Dirk Elliot Tile Co. DE
6382 East Utah Avenue
Spokane, WA 99212
888-245-7248
dirkelliottile.com
Artistic ceramics in beautiful colors.

Duca di Camastra DUC
CP 91
San Stefano di Camastra,
Italy 98077
011-39-0921-339241
ducadicamastra.it
Hand-painted Italian ceramic and terra-cotta tiles.

Dune USA DU
4849 Dawing Road, Unit 1
Jacksonville, FL 32207
904-739-9300
dune.es
Modern ceramic, glass, and eco-friendly offerings made in Brazil.

Edelman Leather EL
80 Pickett District Road
New Milford, CT 06776
860-350-9600
Additional locations in Atlanta;
Boston; Chicago; Dallas; Dania
Beach, Florida; Los Angeles;
New York; San Francisco; and
Washington, D.C.
edelmanleather.com
Leather tiles in myriad colors, sizes, and finishes. To the trade only.

Edilgres-Sirio Ceramiche EG
Via Ghiarola Vecchia 19
Fiorano Modenese, Italy 41042
011-39-0536-816311
edilgres-sirio.it
Modern and classic ceramic and porcelain.

Eleek, Inc. EI
2326 North Flint Avenue
Portland, OR 97227
503-232-5526
eleekinc.com
Recycled-aluminum tiles in an assortment of metal-colored finishes.

Eliane Ceramic Tiles ECT
1500 Luna Road, Suite 106
Carrollton, TX 75006
972-481-7854
elianeusa.com
Brazilian manufacturer of high-style porcelain.

Etruria Design ED
Via Jugoslavia 74/76
Modena, Italy 41100
011-39-059-452188
etruriadesign.it
Mod glazed ceramics in classic beveled shapes and bright hues.

Floor Gres FG
Via Canaletto 24
Fiorano Modenese, Italy 41042
011-39-0536-840111
floorgres.it
A vast assortment of through-body porcelains mimicking stone and metal.

Gayafores GA
Apdo Correos 36
Onda, Spain 12200
011-34-964-626-262
gayafores.es
Glazed ceramic by a venerable maker.

Granada Tiles GT
1109 West Kensington Road
Los Angeles, CA 90026
213-482-8070
granadatiles.com
Cement tiles manufactured in Nicaragua using environmentally friendly processes.

Hastings Tile & Bath Collection HTB
150 East 58th Street, 10th Floor
New York, NY 10155
212-674-9700
Additional locations; visit the website for a showroom and dealer locator.
hastingstilebath.com
Known for its elegant survey of contemporary porcelain, ceramic, and glass tiles from Italy, Spain, and the United States.

Iznik Tiles and Ceramic Corporation IZ
Kurucesme, Öksüz Çocuk Souk, Number 14
Besiktas, Istanbul, Turkey 80220
011-90-212-287-3243
iznik.com
Quartz-based tiles made using ancient methods.

Jason Miller Studio JMS
843 Meeker Avenue, 2nd Floor
Brooklyn, NY 11222
millerstudio.us
Handmade ceramic composition tiles shaped like cargo containers.

Kronos KR
Via Monte Bianco 3
Fiorano Modenese, Italy 41042
011-39-0536-927711
kronosceramiche.it
A range of contemporary ceramics in pop-art prints and lustrous glazes.

La Moderna Manifattura LMM
Via Don P. Borghi 5
S. Antonino, Italy, 42013
011-39-0536-990177
ecoceramica.com
Traditional and contemporary ceramics.

Lea Ceramiche LC
c/o Lea North America
800 Clanton Road
Charlotte, NC 28217
704-522-6300
ceramichelea.com
Striking ceramic and porcelain by cutting-edge artists and designers.

Made a Mano MAM
Kongensgade 36-38, Floor 1
Copenhagen, Denmark 1264
011-45-33-121-080
madeamano.com
Intensely colored lavastone and hand-painted cotto tiles marrying ancient craftsmanship with modern aesthetics.

Majorca MA
Via del Bosco 26
Scandiano, Italy 42019
011-39-0522764511
majorca.it
Glazed and through-body porcelain.

Marca Corona MC
Via Emilia Romagna 7
Sassuolo, Italy 41049
011-39-0536-867200
marcacorona.it
Stylish and innovative options including ceramics embedded with carbon fiber.

Matter MAT
405 Broome Street
New York, NY 10013
212-343-2600
mattermatters.com
Edgy design boutique offering design tiles by venerable Dutch manufacturer Royal Tichelaar Makkum.

Maya Romanoff MR
1730 West Greenleaf
Chicago, IL 60626
773-465-6909
mayaromanoff.com
Wall coverings and metal tiles.

MIO MIO
340 North 12th Street, Unit 301
Philadelphia, PA 19107
215-925-9359
mioculture.com
From an eco-friendly design company, easy-to-install unfinished cork tiles for walls and floors in graphic shapes.

ModCraft MOD
718-541-1160
mod-craft.com
Bold stoneware relief tiles by an architect-turned–product designer.

Motawi Tileworks MT
170 Enterprise Drive
Ann Arbor, MI 48103
734-213-0017
motawi.com
*Run by a pair of siblings, the studio
follows Arts and Crafts traditions with
hand-applied polychrome glazes and
ornamental patterns.*

Native Trails NT
4173 Santa Fe Road, Suite A
San Luis Obispo, CA 93401
800-786-0862
nativetrails.net
*Hammered copper tiles and sprightly
hand-painted Mexican-style ceramics.*

Nemo Tile Company NTC
48 East 21st Street
New York, NY 10010
212-505-0009
800-636-6845
nemotile.com
*Multi-line showroom featuring stone,
ceramic, glass, and eco-friendly
selections plus a portfolio of high-design
porcelains.*

Novoceram NO
ZI Orti, Laveyron BP20
Saint Vallier Sur Rhône, Cedex,
France 26241
011-33-475-235-023
novoceram.fr
*Ceramic tiles made by a century-old
producer.*

Oceanside Glasstile OG
glasstile.com
Visit website for dealer locations.
*Designers' go-to source for lush, eco-
friendly glass mosaics and tiles.*

Peronda PER
Avenida Manuel Escobedo, 26
Onda, Spain 12200
011-964-60-20-12
peronda.com
*Porcelain in woodlike and faux-metal
looks.*

Petracer's Ceramics PC
Via Ghiorola Nuova 228
Fiorano Modenese, Italy 41042
011-39-0536-812163
petracer.it
*Glamorous, fashion-forward ceramics
with elegant graphics and gilded
accents.*

Popham Design PD
323-906-9556
pophamdesign.com
*Handmade Moroccan cement tiles in
chic modern graphics.*

Ragno RA
V. le Virgilio 30
Modena, Italy 41100
011-39-059-384111
ragno.it
*Glazed porcelain in eye-catching colors
and oversized formats.*

Rex Ceramiche Artistiche RCA
Via Canaletto 24
Fiorano Modenese, Italy 41042
011-39-0536-840111
rex-cerart.it
*Luxurious porcelain, glass, and
ceramics.*

SensiTile Systems SEN
1604 Clay Street, Suite 133
Detroit, MI 48211
313-872-6314
sensitile.com
*Fiber-optic enhanced concrete and
acrylic polymer tiles.*

Sicis SI
470 Broome Street
New York, NY 10013
877-839-8900
Additional locations in Chicago
sicis.com
*Glamorous mosaics—including
oversized wallpaper patterns—in glass,
steel, gold, iridium, marble, and
waterglass.*

Stone Source SS
215 Park Avenue South
New York, NY 10003
212-979-6400
Locations in Boston; Chicago;
Los Angeles; Philadelphia;
Washington, D.C.
stonesource.com
*An encyclopedic resource of natural and
engineered stones as well as terrazzo,
glass, ceramics, metals, and porcelains.*

Studio Le Nid SLN
Via Fonte Maimonide 119
Paterno, Sicily, Italy 95047
011-39-95-854125
lenid.it
*Masterfully crafted, hand-painted
ceramics in geometric shapes and
traditional motifs.*

Tanimar TAN
Via Monchio 3
Fiorano Modenese, Italy 41042
011-39-0536-911405
tanimar.it
Ceramic, stone, and marble tiles.

Ticsa America TIC
386 Cliffwood Park
Brea, CA 92821
714-671-7939
ticsa.net
*An incredible assortment of Spanish-
style terra-cotta tiles with beautifully
antiqued patinas.*

Trend USA TR
2700 Biscayne Boulevard
Miami, FL 33137
305-593-6027
trendgroup-usa.com
*Design-forward Italian-made glass
mosaics, ceramics, and agglomerates
with an eco-friendly twist.*

Trikeenan Tileworks TT
P.O. Box 22
Keene, NH 03431
603-355-2961
trikeenan.com
*Renowned for exquisite glazes, this
artisanal outfit makes lush ceramics
according to Arts and Crafts traditions
in an eco-friendly manner.*

Tulikivi TU
Visit website for distributors.
tulikivi.com
Soapstone tiles in a range of colors and sizes, sourced from Finland.

Urban Archaeology UA
143 Franklin Street
New York, NY 10013
urbanarchaeology.com
A bevy of upscale offerings, from exotic marble mosaics to handcrafted terra-cotta.

Valpanaro Candia VAL
S/S 467 Number 128
S. Antonino Cosalgran, Italy 42013
011-39-0536-821111
valpanaro-candia.it
High-tech porcelain and mosaics.

Vidrotil Mosaico VI
Through Tile Trade
3220 N Street NW, Suite 137
Washington, DC 20007
202-470-0487
vidrotil.com
Handmade glass mosaics with incredible depth and color.

Walker Zanger WZ
1050 Amboy Avenue
Perth Amboy, NJ 08861
732-697-7700
Additional locations: 16 throughout the United States.
walkerzanger.com
Multi-line stone and tile showroom offering a comprehensive assortment of styles.

Xenia Taler Design XT
3884 Chesswood Drive
North York, Ontario
Canada M3J 2W6
416-588-8950
xeniataler.com
Hand-painted ceramic tiles detailed with whimsical imagery.

ARTISANS

In addition to the showrooms and manufacturers listed within the guide, there are countless tile makers for you to consider. Below are some of our favorites.

MULTILINE SHOWROOMS

Country Floors
15 East 16th Street
New York, NY 10003
212-627-8300
Visit website for additional locations across the country.
countryfloors.com
The website also has a great online glossary.

Dal-Tile
Visit the website for dealer locations.
daltile.com
One of the largest American manufacturers, offering a vast selection of tile in a full complement of materials and formats.

Modwalls
831-439-9734
modwalls.com
Online showroom selling a wide range of glass, ceramic, cork, and stone tile options.

Paris Ceramics
150 East 58th Street, 7th Floor
New York, NY 10155
212-644-2782
Additional locations in Atlanta; Boston; Chicago; Greenwich, Connecticut; Los Angeles; Naples, Florida; Palm Beach; San Francisco; and Washington, D.C.
parisceramics.com
Reclaimed and newly quarried stone as well as terra-cotta and ceramics.

Renaissance Tile & Bath
349 Peachtree Hills Avenue
Atlanta, GA 30305
404-231-9203
Additional locations in Charlotte; Dallas; Nashville; and Washington, D.C.
renaissancetileandbath.com
A wide range of artisanal options.

Shelly Tile
979 Third Avenue
New York, NY 10022
212-832-2255
Luxurious offerings in ceramic and stone.

Soli
32 NE 39th Street
Miami, FL 33137
305-573-4860
soliusa.com
Exotic surfaces in an array of materials.

Studium
150 East 58th Street, 7th Floor
New York, NY 10155
212-486-1811
studiumnyc.com
Stones, mosaics, and ceramics.

Tile Shop
Visit the website for locations.
tileshop.com
A large selection of stone—from granite to marble—as well as ceramic, porcelain, and glass at a variety of price points.

Waterworks
800-899-6757
Visit the website for nearest location.
waterworks.com
Beloved by designers, this upscale company crafts a lovely assortment of stylish ceramics and glass and sells myriad exotic stones.

ARTS & CRAFTS

Pewabic Pottery
10125 East Jefferson Avenue
Detroit, MI 48214
313-822-0954
pewabic.com
Museum and workshop housed in a 1907 Tudor Revival building that's designated a National Historic Landmark.

Pratt & Larson
Visit the website for dealer locations.
prattandlarson.com
Beautifully handmade, hand-glazed ceramics, many embellished with whimsical motifs.

CONTEMPORARY CERAMICS AND PORCELAIN

Ceramica Magica
Via Padre Sacchi 42
Scandiano, Italy 42019
011-39-0522-851000
cermagica.it
High-tech and refined porcelain.

Colli
Via Viazza 1, Tronco 42
Fiorano Modenese, Italy 41042
011-39-0536-839311
colli.it
Sleek and contemporary porcelain.

Elle-G Ceramiche
Via A. Volta 7
Villalunga di Casalgrande, Italy 42013
011-39-0522-772511
gambinigroup.it
Ceramic tiles for walls and floors.

Fiordo Industrie Ceramiche
Via Emilia Romagna 31
Sassuolo, Modena, Italy 41049
011-39 0536 814811
fiordo.it
Glazed and stonelike porcelain and mosaics.

Gambarelli
S.S. 569 224
Solignano, Italy 41050
011-39-059-7577511
gambarelli.it
Porcelain stoneware and mosaics.

Immagine
Via Tazio Nuvolari 15 Maranello, Italy 41053
011-39-0536-943877
immaginestudioimmagine.com
A breadth of offerings in ceramics.

Impronta Italgraniti USA
7200 Fullerton Road
Springield, VA 22150
703-455-9000
improntaitalgranitiusa.com
Porcelain and ceramic, including oversized formats and textile patterns.

Manifattura Emiliana
Via A. Volta 7
Villalunga di Casalgrande, Italy 42013
011-39-0522-772511
gambinigroup.it
State-of-the-art high-fired porcelain.

Marazzi USA
359 Clay Road
Sunnyvale, TX 75182
972-226-0110
marazzitile.com
marazzigroup.com
A variety of design-forward and high-performance glazed ceramics, glass, and natural stone.

Monina Ceramica
Via Flaminia Z.I. Nord
Gualdo Tadino, Italy 06023
011-39-075-91471
tagina.it
Streamlined wall and floor tiles in glazed and unglazed porcelain.

Panaria
Via Panaria Bassa 22/A
Finale Emilia, Italy 41034
011-39-0535-95111
panaria.it
Ceramic wall and floor tiles, glazed porcelain, and mosaics.

Sole Mio
Gambarelli Group
S.S. 569 224
Solignano, Italy 41050
011-39-059-7577511
gambarelli.it
Colorful ceramics with rich glazes and hand-painted details.

Tau Cerámica
Quadra La Torta 2
Castellón, Spain 12006
011-964-25-01-05
tauceramic.net
Mod ceramics and porcelains in forward-thinking styles.

CORK

American Cork
888-955-2675
amcork.com
Floor and wall tiles in styles ranging from variegated earth tones to rich blues and greens.

Cork Concepts
P.O. Box 100148
North Shore Mail Centre
Auckland, New Zealand
011-64-9-44-33-134
corkconcepts.com
Cork in bold colors and metallic finishes plus unexpected formats such as elongated planks and oversized squares.

Duro Design Flooring
4656 Louis B. Mayer Street
Laval, Canada QC H7P 6E4
888-528-8518
duro-design.com
Bamboo, engineered wood, and other eco options, including a breadth of cork flooring.

Expanko
1129 West Lincoln Highway
Coatesville, PA 19320
800-345-6202
expanko.com
High-quality cork flooring—including wildly flecked patterns—plus floating cork floor systems and rubber tiles.

Globus Cork
741 East 136th Street
Bronx, NY 10454
corkfloor.com
Great selection of corks in unique and made-to-order sizes.

Wicanders
Visit website for store locations.
wicanders.com
Refined offerings for walls and floors, including woodlike planks.

ECO-FRIENDLY TILES

Coverings, Etc.
138 Spring Street, 6th Floor
New York, NY 10012
212-625-9393
Additional locations in Miami and Palm Beach.
coveringsetc.com
An assortment of eco-friendly tiles, agglomerates, and natural stones.

Heath Ceramics
400 Gate 5 Road
Sausalito, CA 94965
415-332-3732
heathceramics.com
Beautifully glazed stoneware in midcentury modern styles.

LEATHER

Inpelle
Via Strà 100
Belfiore, Italy 37050
011-39-045-614-5222
High-end Italian leather tiles with magnetized backing systems in a range of designs.

Interior Leather Surfaces
5 Lakeshore Close
Sleepy Hollow, NY 10591
877-231-2100
leathertile.com

MOSAICS

Erin Adams Design
1204 Fourth Street
Albuquerque, NM 87102
505-352-1016
erinadamsdesign.com
Also a textile designer and fine artist, Adams handcrafts glass and metal mosaics in cheerful patterns as well as glass-inlaid concrete tiles.

Mosaic House
62 West 22nd Street
New York, NY 10010
212-414-2525
mosaichse.com
Moroccan-style mosaics. To the trade.

New Ravenna Mosaics
P.O. Box 1000
Exmore, VA 23350
757-442-3379
newravenna.com
One of the most creative ateliers, run by artisan Sara Baldwin, whose designs range from tiger prints to classical motifs.

Serpentile
212-427-4232
serpentile.home.mindspring.com
Mosaic artisan whose handiwork can be seen enlivening the New York City subway system in addition to high-end homes across the country.

RECLAIMED STONES

Ditta Medici
Via Papareschi 32
Rome, Italy 00146
011-39-06-556-1646
dittamedici.it
A 170-year-old family-owned company renowned for fine marble quarried from around the world plus an inventory of antique marble varieties dating as old as 2,000 years.

Exquisite Surfaces
150 East 58th Street, 9th floor
New York, NY 10155
212-355-7990
Plus additional locations
xsurfaces.com
New stones in distressed patinas, hand-painted decorative ceramics, and salvaged stones.

Old World Stone
1151 Heritage Road
Burlington, Ontario
Canada L7L 4V1
905-332-5547
oldworldstone.com
Specializes in stone restoration for historic buildings.

SPECIALTY ITEMS

Above View
4750 South Tenth Street
Milwaukee, WI 53221
414-744-7118
aboveview.com
Plaster ceiling tiles.

Decorative Cast Basalt
P.O. Box 109
Webster Springs, WV 26288
304-619-7585
decorativebasalt.com
Cast basalt tiles.

Decorative Imaging
281 West Cedar Street
Norwalk, CT 06854
614-352-0745
decorativeimaging.net
Digitally printed parquet floor tiles.

Euramex, Inc.
305-668-4242
Reproduction encaustic tiles.

Get Real Surfaces
212-414-1620
getrealsurfaces.com
Custom concrete tile and specialty surfaces.

Imagine Tile
100 Delawanna Avenue, 5th Floor
Clifton, NJ 07014
973-771-0987
imaginetile.com
Digitally printed ceramic tiles.

Kiln Enamel
Visit the website for dealers.
kilnenamel.com
To-the-trade-only enameled copper tiles.

Robin Reigi Art & Objects
48 West 21st Street
New York, NY 10010
212-924-5558
robin-reigi.com
Unusual and innovative specialty surfaces—including resin, rubber, and eco-friendly tiles—sold exclusively to the trade.

Solistone
18409 East Valley Boulevard
La Puente, CA 91744
800-246-2156
solistone.com
River-rock mosaics, metal tiles, stone, and glass.

STONE

Charles Luck Stone Center
804-282-7990
804-641-2580
charlesluck.com
A selection of stones sourced from across the globe, handcrafted using Old World methods.

Estefano Reiser Floors
786-218-8459
estefanoreiser@aol.com
French limestone and other popular stones.

Intarsia
9550 Satellite Boulevard, Suite 180
Orlando, FL 32837
407-859-5800
intarsiainc.com
Stone mosaic medallions and borders.

STUDIO ARTISANS

Coral Bourgeois
545 Pawtucket Avenue
Pawtucket, RI 02860
401-435-5571
coralbourgeois.com
Fun, whimsically embellished ceramics by a jewelry designer turned tile artisan.

Dominic Crinson
27 Camden Passage
Islington, London UK N1 8EA
011-44-207-704-6538
crinson.com
Digitally printed ceramic tiles in bold patterns.

Flux Studios
4001 North Ravenswood Avenue, Unit 603
Chicago, Illinois 60613
773-883-2030
fluxstudios.com
Stainless-steel and bronze tiles plus wood mosaics handmade from sustainable solid bamboo, teak, and rosewood.

Oldsjö Hultgren Design
oldsjohultgrendesign.se
Quirky shapes from a pair of Swedish designers.

Sonoma Tilemakers
Check the website for dealers.
sonomatilemakers.com
Handcrafted ceramics and metals.

Trout Studios
227 Turkey Drive
Dripping Springs, TX 78620
512-894-0774
troutstudios.com
Decorative metal tiles.

TERRA-COTTA

Saint Tropez Stone Boutique
25 Evelyn Way
San Francisco, CA 94127
415-513-5920
sainttropezstone.com
Moorish, terra-cotta, and encaustic cement tiles with Middle Eastern flair.

OTHER SPECIALTY RESOURCES

Additional organizations, companies, and places of interest.

RADIANT HEATING

Nu-Heat
860-778-9276
nuheat.com

Suntouch
888-432-8932
suntouch.net

Uponor
800-321-4739
uponor-usa.com

Warmboard Radiant Subfloor
831-685-9276
warmboard.com

ASSOCIATIONS AND NONPROFITS

The Aluminum Association
703-358-2988
aluminum.org

Building Stone Institute
866-786-6313
buildingstoneinstitute.org

Ceramic Tiles of Italy Association
italiantiles.com
s-tiles.it

Interlocking Concrete Paving Institute
icpi.org

Marble Institute of America
320-230-0728
marble-institute.com

National Association of Homebuilders
nahb.com

National Kitchen & Bath Association
800-842-6522
nkba.com

National Terrazzo and Mosaic
Association
540-751-0930
ntma.com

National Tile Contractors
Association
P.O. Box 13629
Jackson, MS 39236
601-939-2071
tile-assn.com

Natural Stone Council
800-210-3916
genuinestone.com

The Radiant Panel Association
800-660-7187
radiantpanelassociation.org

Society of American Mosaic
Artists
866-902-7262
americanmosaics.org

Tile Council of North America
864-646-8453
tileusa.com

Tile Heritage Foundation
707-431-8453
tileheritage.org

Tiles of Spain
spaintiles.info

U.S. Green Building Council
800-795-1747
usgbc.org

CULTURAL ATTRACTIONS

Iznik Tile Foundation and
Research Center
Kurucesme, Oksuz, Cocuk SK,
No. 14
Istanbul, Turkey 80220
011-90-212-287-3243
iznik.com
*This working studio and shop provides
a behind-the-scenes peek at how
artisans are reviving the art of quartz-
based tile making.*

National Tile Museum of Lisbon
(Museu Nacional Do Azulejo)
Rua da Madre de Deus, 4
Lisbon, Portugal 1900-312
011-351-218-100-34
mnazulejo-ipmuseus.pt
Historic Portuguese ceramics.

Pewabic Pottery Museum
10125 East Jefferson Avenue
Detroit, MI 48214
313-822-0954
pewabic.com
*The studio, established in 1903,
encompasses a museum and a
nonprofit arts-education foundation
teaching visitors about Arts and Crafts
tile-making traditions.*

Acknowledgments

This book would not have been possible without the contributions of innumerable specialists and supporters. First and foremost, thank you to my editor, Aliza Fogelson, who dreamed up the project, made it come to life, and made me a better writer and thinker in the process. I am grateful to Doris Cooper for the opportunity to work with the talented team at Clarkson Potter, and to Samantha Nestor for the introduction.

Any design effort—whether building a home or assembling a 320-page book—is a balance between big-picture vision and attention to minute details, and *The Art of Tile* is no exception. A huge thanks to Wayne Wolf, whose elegant design made these pages both delectable and navigable, and to Jane Treuhaft at Clarkson Potter for her creative direction, thoroughness, and—above all—patience (which I know was tested by 2,000 photographs of tile!).

I am especially indebted to my collaborator, Ben Ritter, for his evocative photographs and unflagging professionalism, and for knowing when to lighten the mood. Damaris Colhoun's invaluable research assistance also helped broaden the book's scope and depth of coverage.

Many people fall in love with tile after being exposed to the painstaking artistry behind hand-glazed terra-cotta or exquisitely crafted ceramics. I, however, became enamored with the medium from quite the opposite direction, seduced by state-of-the-art porcelains. For this I owe Chris Abbate, the entire Novita staff (particularly Danielle De Vita), and the extended Ceramic Tiles of Italy family for sending me across the globe and into the sanctums of some of the most cutting-edge manufacturers.

I'd like to extend a heartfelt thanks to those who provided access to the lovely homes featured within these pages—and to the designers of those spaces for letting me pick their brains. Many showrooms generously provided access to their stunning inventories, including Ann Sacks, Edelman Leather, Hastings Tile & Bath, Stone Source, Trend USA, and Urban Archaeology. A special acknowledgment goes to Matt Karlin and Raymond Moore of Nemo Tile for technical insight and support, to Echo Mackenzie of Edelman Leather for her buoyant spirit, and to Artistic Tile's Nancy Epstein and Jan MacLatchie for encouragement.

Throughout the writing process, Jessica Olshen and Annie Block provided constant fortification with food, wine, and positive thoughts. To Ginger and Bobby: thanks for all the love and cheerleading I could ask for and then some. And, lastly, I am indebted to Carlos Salgado for so many things, most especially for keeping me sane and focused. Thank you beyond words for being a constant source of design inspiration and love.

Index